Black Sheep Walk

Diane M. Mahone

Trigger warning: This book contains stories that may be distressing, disheartening, uncomfortable, and controversial. The publisher, the staff, nor the author intend to offend anyone who reads this book. This book was published for the sole purpose of healing, and we pray that it will be received as such.

Acknowledgments

First and foremost, I thank the Holy Spirit and Jesus Christ for endowing me with the wisdom and courage to write this book to not only free my soul but also the souls of many others!

I want to thank all three of my beautiful angels; Trey, Keniya, and Kaydence for being my strength as I stayed up long nights and sacrificed hours away from them. Thank you for loving me through it all.

I want to thank my God Mother, Mrs. Pearly Keith, for instilling in me Matthew 6:33 at the young tender age of 15 to ***"Seek ye first the kingdom of God and His righteousness, and all these things shall be added unto you!"***
Thank you for all the wisdom, teaching me how to dress like a classy lady, and act like the woman of God I was created to be. Thank you for always believing in me and what God put in me.

I want to thank my best friend Lauren for being there through thick and thin and through many trials of my life you were there to listen, encourage and give me sound advice. I love you always.

I want to thank all my friends that have motivated and believed in me throughout my journey; Miranda, my sisters, Bethany, Destinee, Jessica, Jess, all my favorite cousins, and all of you who have a special place in my heart.

I want to give a special shoutout to my poetry family, you know who you are. If it wasn't for you all being so brave and courageous to speak your truth unapologetically, I wouldn't have picked up the pen to ever write, so thank you and I love you all!

Thank you to all of the leaders, Pastors, and Prophets that have ever given me a prophetic word; including one that I would write a book one day. Thank you for the words you have spoken over me. I am a fulfillment of God's promises! I love you all!

Table of Contents

"I was born with crack in my system, rejection in my spirit, abandonment in my bones, and a will to live. I was born through the womb of rejection and abandonment to break the cycle."

Diane M. Mahone

Does Anybody Want Me?

"Congratulations! It's a girl! What do you want to name her", the nurse asked as she began cleaning the brand-new baby girl, preparing to place her in her mother's arms. "I don't care what it is, I don't want to hold it, I don't want it. You name her," the woman replied as she looked away, making sure not to have eye contact with the baby or the nurse. "Would you like to see her before I put her in the incubator? She's beautiful." "No. I didn't want the other ones and I don't want this one either."

The nurse was in utter shock. She figured she would try one last time. She had seen cases like this before, but it was always heartbreaking to hear. "Are you sure? Can we get you some assistance that can help you?" The woman continued to tell the nurse no until she finally gave up.

With tears in her eyes, the nurse said a faint, "Ok", and walked out of the room with the baby. She walked back to the nursery and put the brand new baby girl in the incubator. "What are we going to name you beautiful?" At that moment, she looked down and there was a magazine on the table beside her that read, Princess Dianna. "Dianna? Do you like that? Well, you sure are a princess and one day you will be a Queen."

I was born in Harlem hospital on July 1, 1987, 2 months early. I came into the world a fighter and I've been fighting ever since. Unlike most children who went home with their parents, bubbling with joy from their newborn's arrival, my mother did not want me. I was born into a world without an identity and no clue as to where I would even begin to find it.

After traveling up and down the east coast with different families, my sister and I were finally placed in a permanent family by an agency out of Yonkers, New York. At the tender age of 5 years old I was finally adopted into this new family. In my new family, I was the middle child of three. The woman also had two other children in her home at the same time. There was an older boy who was 12 and a little girl my age.

Immediately, the older boy was removed from the home. He never knew why, but I was removed from my previous home because of an older man putting his hands in places they shouldn't have ever been. I was only a toddler when this happened! Because of that, my caseworker never allowed me to be in a home with adult men or male children or over 12. After they removed him, me, my biological sister and, my other newly adopted sister were the only children living in the house with my adopted mother and her sister.

I was always talking, when not spoken to and when I did talk, I was told that I talked too much. I was told I had that "middle child syndrome." I've always had a problem with my mouth, and even though I didn't know at that young age then, my mouth and what I spoke would soon change the lives of others for the good! Even at a young age, I believed in standing up for myself, even when no one else did.

"People will forget what you said, people will forget what you did, but people will never forget how you made them feel."
Maya Angelou

I knew I had been in multiple foster homes by this age. Even though I was only 5, I always felt like I didn't belong. It was a sense of feeling alone. I looked different, talked differently and I acted differently. I was skinny, a late bloomer, and my teeth were huge. I was always told to stop smiling because it was "ugly". Well, I happened to think this "ugly" smile was all I had. I was always told as a child that I was bad, and I wasn't going to amount to anything.

As I finally began to settle into my new family and obtain some kind of identity, I quickly found out that some people are very cold inside. I thought that I was receiving a home because someone wanted to love me, and we would have a happy family. On the contrary, she didn't love anyone, including herself.

My adopted mother made it very clear to me at a young age that I was nothing more than a check. She signed my birth certificate and her divorce papers in the same month. Ultimately, she lost her husband's love and his income. I couldn't possibly replace his love, so, I guess money would have to do, for now. I remember thinking to myself, "Shouldn't this love thing work both ways? Shouldn't I have received both love AND security?" She ended up giving her ex-husband rights to me, which he never wanted or earned. He had built a whole different family across town during their marriage, which is why he left. In 14 years, I saw him a handful of times.

My adopted mother was older, somewhere in her fifties. She was brown-skinned, she stood 5'9, her hands were rough, her knuckles were swollen because she cleaned rich white folk's homes for a living, and she suffered from arthritis. We always had nice clothes and new bikes every few months. My mother also had a bad gambling problem. She loved scratch-offs, "playing her numbers", lottery tickets, and her favorite out of all of them was Bingo! It wasn't the safest place. It was a Bingo

Hall. What some would call, a "hole in the wall", in Jamaica-Queens, NY.

I'll never forget being hungry and stuck in a back seat with my two other sisters. We were told if we unlock the doors to her old, raggedy, beat-up Cadillac, she will break whoever's fingers that did it. Maybe she didn't say the old raggedy part, but I knew it was going to be my fingers being broken when she said it! Upon hour six of being in the backseat, we were hungry, tired, and not to mention cold. I decided to be the brave one to go against what she said. I climbed across the front seat into the driver's seat hitting my right knee on the lock of the steering wheel that kept the car on lock. I unlocked the door, stomped my hungry little self into the Bingo Hall where I saw drunk, old, white, and black ladies. I scanned the room looking for my mommy just to tell her we were hungry.

To no surprise, she found me before I found her. She snatched me up by my arm and dragged me across the floor, scraping my knees while cursing me out and wailing and hitting on me at the same time saying, "Didn't......I...tell….....you…....if …YOU..GET…OUT…OF..THIS….CAR..I WILL BREAK YOUR FINGERS!" I screamed loudly, helplessly, hoping someone would hear my tender six-year-old voice crying out, "But we are hungry mommy! She said, "I don't care" while throwing me in the back seat on top of one of my sisters. They were already used to me getting all the beatings while they just watched.

This was the story of my life as a child. I could never be myself. I was always told I talked too much, and I got popped in my mouth for being myself. My mouth was being muzzled little by little as I grew up. I believe this is where the first seed of "I'm not good enough" was planted. After being the sacrifice, we did get McDonald's cheeseburgers with water. Then we went back to the same spot for the rest of the night.

I shared a room with my adopted younger sister. We were the same age. Since I was now separated from my older sister, I started creating a bond with my new sister. She was the opposite of me. She was pretty, light-skinned, and quiet. I was brown skin, boney, and my hair was kinky. Not to mention, I was born with a few holes in my heart as well. I remember going to see the heart doctor growing up. They hooked me up to the E.K.G machines, with l.e.d.s, connected from my head to my feet. I would often overhear the doctor telling my mother I could never be a normal child and this condition may get worse if I did sports or strenuous activities. So not only did I feel ugly, but I also felt disabled. Not to mention, she had long hair. Mine was long, but not as long as my sisters. My mother dressed us like we were twins all the way until middle school. I hated it and she hated it too. We didn't look anything alike, nor did we act alike. I was the life of the party, goofy, and loved to dance.

My sister was like a tomboy and quiet. She loved drawing and singing behind closed doors! Sometimes it was like she wanted to be like me and do everything I did, but she couldn't. I didn't mind telling her she couldn't, which caused me and her to fight, A LOT! I'll never forget one of our worst fights where I ended up on top of her with my hands wrapped around her throat, suffocating her with a pillow, wishing she would die. When my mother found us, she pulled me off of her. "Strip down naked and get in this tub," she said as she stormed down the stairs flying out the back door getting the biggest, spikiest switch she could find.

I could hear her footsteps getting closer as she returned. The closer she got, the more I gripped the sides of the tub. She beat me over and over while telling me she never wanted me, but she needed the money, and how much I was the ugly one. The only reason I was there was that they had no room for me and not to mention how my sister was prettier than me. Her last and final statement shook me to my core. "If I catch your raggedy hands on her again, I will kill you!" I believed her. This was one of 100 whippings that I obtained for doing little to nothing.

I wanted to tell her we were only fighting because I won the dance contest. I screamed and cried and screamed but to no avail, as she left me, my brown skin began to show the result of the beating I had just endured. My tender skin began to welt up. I got out of the tub to see my sister sitting outside of the bathroom door. I stepped out of the tub and grabbed my towel. I started to pat my bruised and battered skin dry. With my head down, attempting to hold in my tears, I walked by her and went into the room to put my pajamas on. She looked sad but she didn't say anything.

Climbing up the bunk bed, getting into bed tossing and turning all night thinking, "Will it always be like this?" I thought, "I don't belong here. This isn't LOVE!" From the way I was treated at home, I grew very REBELLIOUS. I didn't listen to any adult. I would challenge everything they said to me and it would lead to me getting a beating every single day. Sometimes my mother would say, "Girl you should be tired of getting your butt whooped." I was tired, but I was more angry than tired.

The Boy Is Mine

My mother wasn't a churchgoer but when we were young, she would get me, and my sisters dressed in our best Sunday dresses with matching dress socks and matching prayer clothes pinned on our head for a covering (we grew up in an apostolic church). She would drop us off at the church doorsteps. I was confused. "Aren't you supposed to come inside with us," I asked? I wouldn't get an answer. I would just get slapped right in my mouth. I guess that was the answer.

The church people became family. It was a home away from home for me. I had adopted family there. My mother, sister, Mrs. Evette, who was my mother's older sister, and her son, BJ; was the guitar player. She was married, but her husband was a drunk. I never really seen a man in my youth do right by his wife. This stuck with me. We had to sit with my Aunt, and she would always pinch me if I started acting up. I also had a bad habit of laughing at people in the church. I always got pinched. I loved going to church. It was really the only time my mother let us do normal things with kids our age. I had friends there, but they never asked where my mommy or daddy was, and I never told them. I began to sing in the sunshine choir and although I couldn't sing, I still loved it.

As I grew older my mother put us in ballet, tap, karate, and dance. I thought it was because she believed in me and wanted me to explore my gifts. However, I later found out it was actually because she got more money on my check. After all, we did extra-curricular activities. It also gave her time to be alone and spend more money to play her numbers(lottery). She didn't like me that much anyway, so that was just another way to keep us away from her. She would drop us off at the curb and we had to always go in alone.

Even though it was for a malicious reason, I fell in love with dance. I realized that I loved to dance more than anything. My mother was never present at our church programs, nor did she come to any of my extracurricular activities. Dance gave me my outlet to have fun and feel free. When I danced, I felt free. I could feel the beat in my heart while rhythm held my little hips and the secrets of my soul started to come out! I longed to be free! I longed to be loved, to give the love I felt. When I danced, I loved the attention I had when people would just stare at me. I would have dancing competitions with my best friends, and I would always win.

I participated in school competitions and all the boys in my class would say, "She doesn't have a butt, but she sure can dance. They secretly loved me. That's what I told myself anyway. I couldn't wait for the Valentine's Day dance every year at school. That meant I could jack my top up and roll my skirt up to make it shorter. My mother intentionally bought my clothes sometimes two sizes too big, so it wasn't just me trying to be "sexy". I was so excited to dance with my "first love". He liked me, but I loved him. I remember even at the age of 11, grinding my hips on him, hands on the floor, legs in the air, shaking it all on him! I didn't dance like a little girl my age. I danced nasty, I knew it, and I loved it.

I didn't know it then, but the seed of lust and perversion was passed down in my bloodline and that's probably why my adopted mother was so hard on me, she could see the signs. I knew what sex was before I even knew how to differentiate my shapes and colors, but I knew what shape the male genitalia looked like. I never wanted to have sex, I just had knowledge of something I didn't want. I didn't know how to tie my shoe, but I already had generational soul ties on my back that would chase me down for the next 30 years. I was only 3 years old the first time a man put his hands on me, so what else was going to come out of me except that which had been put in me?

Looking at him, I was saying to myself, "One day you will be mine." The next year, I was devastated. I had gotten into trouble at home and my mother told me that I wouldn't be going to the dance that year. She could've just beat me like any other time I did something wrong, but she couldn't stand to see me happy. I much rather have had that, than to not see the love of my life.

She let my sister go. I knew all my friends were going to be there, including my first love. I remember looking out my window, waiting for my best friend to walk by to let me know how it was, but she didn't walk by that night. The following morning, she came to get me. While we walked the eight blocks just to get to school, I could see the scared look on her face when she arrived.

She was loud and jumping up and down on my front step saying, "Girl, we had mad fun last night, I missed you girl!" I asked, "Who did he dance with?" She started saying who she danced with and began to change the subject while telling me who all was there. I said, "Girl! Who did my boo dance with?" She said, "Um, you know the light-skinned chick he likes from science class? I said, "Oh, her?" She said, "Yea." I asked, "Who else?" "She danced with him all night. Well enough about that, I'm hungry. Let's get a bacon, egg, and cheese bagel and some sunflower seeds from the corner store." She brushed me off as if she didn't just tell me the love of my life had another love!

"Oh, no she didn't", I said as I began to roll up my grey school uniform skirt. I took my hair out from the ugliest big box braids that my mother could give me. She would connect one to the other instead of giving me ponytails or cornrows. She knew it was ugly, and I knew it was ugly. It was another way of her punishing me and making me feel less than pretty. I knew I would be getting a beating when I got home, but I didn't care. I was used to getting them.

When we got to school, I stormed into my homeroom. That's when I saw him, my future love, and he was flirting with her. I will never forget that moment. I remember the thoughts running through my head. I felt like I wasn't pretty enough. I had to compete with the girl to get his attention. The same way I had to compete at home with my sister. My entire world crumbled before my eyes. He was the only happy thing in my life and now he was also attached to another "worst moment of my life."

They spent the rest of middle school dating and as for me, I didn't date anyone for the next 6 years. To be honest I couldn't. He was the first boy I kissed and the first boy I actually liked. I wasn't bringing anyone to meet my mother. She was mean, anyway and she didn't let us have company. I didn't want anyone else at school. I wanted him! So, I ended up alone, again. I had a problem with him being taken from me. It resulted in me having a lack of joy for my early dating years and having fun exploring my youth as most young girls do. It resulted in more rejection and abandonment wounds.

In my house, we had sort of a routine. My mother was very strict when it came down to chores. I had to clean my room, my sister's room, sweep the stairs and rugs, wash the dishes, and most importantly, rake the backyard; until I got blisters on my palms. We never had family time. We never talked about our day. My mother never gave us hugs while telling us she loved us. I did see her tell my younger sister she loved her, and sometimes she would hold her, but not me or my older sister. For a long time, I didn't know I was supposed to receive any of that.

One thing that stood out to me in my home was that sometimes before bed, my mother would call me and my sisters in her bedroom to kneel where we would pray together. When we were done sometimes, she would ask questions about the last home I was in? She would ask me about the scars on my thighs. Like she normally would, she asked me, "Do you remember anything?" I remember my mind traveling back and all I remembered was an older black man in a wheelchair saying, "Come here", and I would yell, "NO!" He would grab on my things and scratch me up. Other than that, it was all a blur. I blocked it out. I would look at my mother with fear and she looked back at me as if she knew more, but she was relieved that I didn't know anymore. Although I didn't know if I was molested or not, I was happy that I was in a home that men couldn't touch me in places that they shouldn't.

My life, as I knew it, was missing something. I had decent clothes, I had a mother(kinda), sisters, an auntie, friends, and an absent father. I was somewhat popular in school, so I had friends. This bully tried me one time, but I won. Before fighting me, she was undefeated. As we sat in the office, waiting on our punishment, she revealed to me that she was also abused. It was at that moment I realized that she became a bully because she was being bullied.

I wasn't lacking anything when it came to people, but I still felt alone. When I laid down at night, I was empty. I didn't feel loved, and I didn't know how to give love. I knew it was something, I just didn't know what. Although I was a sweet little girl with a big personality, I still had a part of me that yearned for a mother's touch; the one that bonds a mother and daughter for life. I never really thought about my dad, I didn't know I was supposed to. My mother was a single mom, so I became accustomed to what I saw growing up. All I have ever known about my birth mother for the first 27 years of my life was that my mother was a crackhead, a prostitute, and she was having babies every year. When I was younger, I often thought about her; what did she look like? Did I look like her? Did she have remorse for leaving me in the hospital? I hoped to one day get answers to these questions that pierced my soul.

See You Later

Sometimes I would hear the whispers between her and my aunt, but I knew to stay out of grown folks' business. I had two other siblings that my mother would take my sister and me to visit. They lived with a lady named Joan. She was also known as our "Grandma". She was much older too. She looked mean on the outside, but I liked her. She had a hunch in her back, a bad hip, and bad knees. She would always tell me that I was a beautiful little girl and I needed to be careful not to become a "fast" child. For those in the newer generation, calling girls "fast" was the same thing as calling a girl a hoe.

I didn't know what that meant at that time, but I listened. I didn't like her husband. He was tall and he was missing an arm. He would sometimes pull on my skirts, dresses, or pants when she wasn't looking. He even hit my butt! I was afraid of what he could do to me, so I always stayed close to my sister. She had a wall of plaques in her house. She said that one of them was of my mother, but I would never look at it. It was at the age of 9 when I realized that my birth mother was in the foster care systems too. I didn't know what that meant then, but now I know I was a part of a generational curse.

Seeing my blood sisters and brothers occasionally growing up, made me feel more blessed than cursed. My baby sister was always kicked out of school or getting into fights. Fighting was in my blood. I came into this world fighting for my life and it followed in my blood. I was told I had 2 older brothers: one looked like me and the other like my older sister. They were never there. When I asked Mrs. Joan about them, I was always told they were back in a group home in Yonkers, NY. It was because they were always in the streets and doing things that weren't good for them. It was a place you would've never wanted to end back up at. My adopted mom would tell me all the time that's where I would end up if I didn't behave.

These visits to Mrs. Joan's home began to grow less and less until I never saw my siblings anymore. All that was left were memories and not the good ones. My sister would always beg to come with me, I loved her so much. I always felt like it was my job to protect her, and I couldn't. She was only a year younger than me, and we shared the same birthday month. I felt helpless because I couldn't be there for her. Sadly, my brothers were too far gone in the streets to even realize they had a sister.

My older sister handled things a lot differently than me. She was the observer; slow to speak. She never really cared whose home she ended up in or who loved her or not. She acted like she didn't need what I did; she was numb. She was the loyal one. No matter what, if she rocked with you, she had your back. Well, she always had my back. She was my bodyguard. She protected me from bullies and boys. She was the smart one; street smart, that is. Her best friends growing up were always boys. She would always get their opinion or learn from their behaviors. We were very close growing up, but I always felt like she would never tell me her biggest secrets, fears, or who she liked. I took it as no one was wise enough or good enough to be with my sister.

I wondered if she knew she was good enough. I thought she was. She was my hero. Everything I went through, she experienced first. She didn't complain like I did, even though I knew she felt the way I did. She always put her best foot forward. She was known around the block for being the cool one, but don't cross her. Her nickname was "one heavy hitter", meaning she hit you one time and you're out. We only got into a fight one time and although she was twice my size, I won. I'll never forget, we were pulling hair, kicking each other, and ripping up each other's shirts like Mike Tyson and Evander Holyfield. She was losing, so she sat on me until I couldn't breathe. I earned points that day. I knew if I could take her out, I could fight. The only thing I didn't like about myself was that when I blacked out, I changed into someone that I didn't like. I became numb and all I could see was black. I knew I would hurt you. I wasn't just an ordinary fighter. It was like I was fighting from deep within. I was afraid of this anger and rage that would show up in me from time to time. I earned the nickname, "light hands". I would slap you even before you could say anything to me, like out of nowhere. If we were fighting, I was pulling something while punching you in your face.

Everything was normal, as normal could be, until one day my mother came home crying. I knew it was bad when she made my younger sister and I go into our room while she called my older cousin, and aunt, in her room. Although I was told not to come out of the room, I wanted to know what was wrong. I snuck down the hallway and listened through the crack of the door. All I could hear her say was, "They found a lump here and there, and surgery would be in a few days." Also, she told them not to tell us because she didn't want us to worry. The next few weeks were rough. When my mother came home from the hospital, there were gauze pads and drains where her breasts once were. She looked like she was in so much pain and I wanted to help her, but she just told me to leave her alone.

After a week or so, while lying in bed she called me into her room and told me that she had cancer. I asked, "Didn't aunt Evevette, die from that a few months ago?" She answered, "Yes. Hers was in her bones and mine is in my breasts." She told me she was undergoing chemotherapy and it would kill the rest of the cancer. Over the next couple of months, I watched her suffer. As my sisters and I ate dinner she would go outside and throw her food up in the backyard. My mother found out in February 1999 and by October 1999 she was gone.

I'll never forget the day she died. Our normal routine was to get dressed to go to school and she would be in the bed looking down the hallway at us. As my sisters went down the stairs, I said, "See you later", like always, and she replied, "Bye, Diane." I looked puzzled but I went to school as normal. Immediately after lunch, my sisters and I received a note instructing us to go to the library because my father would be picking us up. I looked confused because we didn't have a father. I walked to and from school every day with my sisters, so immediately, I knew something was wrong. All of a sudden, I'm not walking home and we are being picked up by someone's "father". This was very strange.

After school, I met my sisters in front of the school. We all looked at each other with fear and confusion in our eyes. We knew something was wrong. We walked 2 blocks to the public library. When we arrived, we saw the man that signed our birth certificate, our adopted father, and he looked a bit sad. My sister ran up to him and hugged him. He then told us all to get in the car. I climbed in the dusty, brown van. I had to sit on work tools as he began to drive. Not knowing how to tell us he said, "Your mother died." So many emotions filled me at that moment. I felt as if my world as I knew it had stopped. My younger sister began to cry, and I just looked down in my lap. I was always good at making people laugh, but this type of feeling was a familiar feeling of pain, so, I did what was common. I stuffed the pain. I was numb. I didn't cry, I just sat there, looking. He drove us to the hospital where my aunt and cousin were.

They were in the home when my mother became ill. I remember the smell of the hospital that day and all the doctors and nurses walking by so quickly. I saw my aunt and cousin pacing the floor as if they were waiting for news. When we came in, they didn't hug me, but they hugged my sisters. More of my cousins begin to arrive from the elevator. They asked if we wanted to see my mother. I replied, "I thought she died?" My aunt interrupted, "No, she's still alive. They have the breathing machine breathing for her right now." Not knowing what that meant, I felt angry and relieved at the same time. So why did He just say she was dead? Probably because he wanted her dead. I was furious because even at that young age I knew the power of what people said.

My sisters went in to visit my mother and came out screaming and crying. Now, it was my turn. My heart was beating so fast, but luckily my older cousin was standing in the hallway and I asked him to go with me, so he did. He always seemed to show up when my mother would talk so much junk about me to his mom. He would show up like he was coming to be the father and discipline me, but he would actually take me to the corner stores where he hung out and let me meet all his cool friends. He would let me get all the junk food I wanted. I loved him and his lifetime partner of almost 20 years of that time. It was the only time I felt normal and cool as a child.

I walked in and saw my mother's body lying there as the breathing machine and tubes pumped air into her lifeless body. Her eyes were wide open, looking at the wall. I broke down for the first time in my life. I cried because even at the age of 13, I knew what death looked like and it had already taken her away. It took my possibility of living a normal life away. With her being gone, I knew she would not suffer anymore, but I felt like I didn't get to bond with her the way I wanted to. All the promises she told me didn't happen. She would never see me get married or have babies! I was assisted back into the waiting room with the rest of the family. At that moment, I was accompanied by fear. Losing the only mom that I knew would affect me. I looked around the room and everyone was heartbroken. I knew my mother, was gone forever.

That night, all my family from South Carolina had arrived. They all just gave hugs and extra hugs. Everyone just looked at me and my sisters like they were more concerned about where we would end up than what was going on. They were fighting about who would get us. My mother had specifically advised them before she died, not to let us get separated.

I missed all my new extended family and I hated only seeing them under these circumstances. I enjoyed seeing my favorite cousins because we all were around the same age and we all spent summers together at my aunt's house in the south.

We all went into my sister's room once we returned home and talked and caught up all night. I spent an hour just picking on how they talked differently from me. They said things like "ain't", "bo", "yes ma'am", and "no sir". I laughed so hard at their accent. At this point, anything to take my mind off what was really going on was good for me. We had girl talk and grubbed on my aunt's homemade smoked sausage sandwiches, that she made in South Carolina and saved it for me until they made it to New York. After that, I was tired. Everyone fell asleep where they were, but I stayed awake. Even as a little girl, I knew when things were not right. Unfortunately, I was always popped in my mouth when I spoke up about those feelings. I felt deep within something haunting me that night. I felt in my stomach that something was going to happen. It was 3:07 am and the house phone rang; twice. My aunt answered the phone and then hung it up a second later.

She came to the bottom of the steps and called our names. "Diane!" I woke my sisters up and we all walked to the steps. She said, "Your mother is gone." My sister began to cry and fall out on the floor. I went and jumped back in my bed quickly. I couldn't feel anything. I walked around for the next few days as if everything was normal. More of our family began to arrive at our house. It was packed both upstairs and downstairs. They did funerals differently in New York at that time. They have funerals in the evening along with the wake. Then, the next morning they would do the burial. It was freezing outside that day as I walked into the church and walked by the casket along with my three sisters.

I froze looking at my sister's collapse then needing assistance on the front row. I couldn't cry. I couldn't feel anything. I turned around and glanced at my family as they looked at me and my sisters. They preached my mother into heaven! Just like most black churches. Ironically, she never even went to church. I never even seen her revere God or pray but she made us do it! I pray she made it in heaven! It was at this moment that I realized I was different again. I didn't want to fake being sad or fake anything. At this point, I had so many emotions inside of me, but I felt no one cared about little ol' me. I just lost my mother and I couldn't cry. To me, that was a problem. Just like most of my problems I just pushed it deeper inside of me.

Once everyone left, two of my mother's sisters stayed behind and I overheard them talking about moving us to South Carolina. They never officially said that I was going. The next few months for me and my sisters were rough; Thanksgiving and Christmas were never the same. We often shared memories that would make us burst out in laughter versus crying. Christmas was my mother's favorite holiday. This was the time of the year that she would get us everything we wanted and more, but tell us we weren't getting anything. I would always sneak into the living room the night before Christmas to see her roll out new bikes. She and my aunt stayed up for hours wrapping gifts and she included all of our names. This was the one time my mother was fair. We always had the same amount of gifts.

We all came downstairs to find a handful of presents wrapped; none of what I nor my sisters wanted. My aunt wasn't kid-friendly, and she didn't like me at all. She always told me from when I was a little girl, that my mouth would get me killed. I feared her and she took advantage of that. She would just hit me as I walked by her. Sometimes, she would tell my mother that I needed a beating for no reason. It was like she enjoyed seeing me scream and holler.

She also wasn't good at showing her emotions. I could tell she did what she could, but let's face it, her sister, our mother, was never going to be seen or heard from again. It all happened so fast. I had tried to live a normal life as a teenager, but with the rumors going around at school that I lost my mother, along with people asking me if I was okay, I just didn't want to break down. "I am strong", I told myself, but deep down, I was afraid. I felt like a motherless child.

RIP to My Adopted Mother(poem)

"I didn't hate her, but I didn't love her either."-Diane

Dear Mama,

Roses are red. Violets are black and blue.

I was a child. You wanted this motherless child.

Signing adoption papers without ink was pointless.

The point is you weren't a good mother to me.

Mothers are nurturers, loving, teachers.

In a box sheltered in my mind.

Sheltered in this world.

You left me.

You labeled my box.

Everything but my name.

I was dormant.

Doormat you were feet.

Stepped on me.

Feet wiping.

Stomped on.

Walked over to get into the house that was never a home.

You kept me isolated in a room, never to be free.

Free?

What is free momma?

I long for the memories too but sometimes not even a brain injury could make you forget.

Like the time I went to my neighbor's house.

I was only six.

I danced so hard I had all the attention on me! I sweated out my clothes.

You couldn't stand to see me happy, so you beat my skin until it raised up like TB shots!

I associated everything good was followed by a letdown.

Beat down to the ground until I pick myself back up again as if it never happened.

I became accustomed to making excuses for people's bad behavior!

Letting people down and beating them down with my words, I followed in your footsteps.

All I ever wanted to tell you was, "I love you."

I just wanted to grab you.

Love all the hell out of youuuuu!

Hugs are all I ever wanted from you mama!

You left me in the box shipped to the next available, you know what?

This is not an easy poem for me this was my life

Y'all can keep remembering childhood and I'll just keep trying to forget.

But I can never forget that one time I ran away from home never to return again.

You sent for the box.

Pick up box, jumped, boxed, and beat with blinds in buckles until box went blind and knees buckled.

I went away into a sunken place.

I wanted to get out!

I died that day.

Mouth open, muzzled, and buried alive by you.

Mind in captivity.

Head trauma!

Then a voice whispered to me, "You shall not die but live!"

I immediately saw myself standing in large crowds.

That's what happens when you have a near-death experience.

It allows you the opportunity to get up. Wake up.

Rising out of that box, I got up!

In a bed with mild concussions and more secrets swept under the bed warrior, I am a warrior!

Champion!

Courageous is who I am.

I wanted to write this from your grave,

But I have never visited it.

It's taken me 18 years to heal.

I forgive you for not being able to show me the love you never received as a child.

I'm sorry you had to grow up without a mother.

In return, I grew up without one either.

I'm in therapy now.

I take my daily dose of forgiveness, I have been reborn.

I went from the dungeon of darkness into the marvelous light.

I am a light.

I awake each day on purpose.

I am a Queen with power in my hands and in my mouth.

I speak life to you never give up!

Never catch feelings but flights, above it all!

Stay above like eagles flying above conflict

State of confusion is distracting

Never be distracted but focus on what's ahead. There's someone that needs you ahead.

Everything happens for a reason, you may not see it now, but you'll thank me later, see it later.

I am walking with words.

Words to heal, words to deliver, one wound at a time through my storyline!

I might forget a lot, but I'll never forget you.

Despite the pain, I loved you anyway.

May you S.I.P. Mom

Welcome to South Carolina

I woke up out of my sleep and there she was. "Aunt Flo", aka, my period. I remembered all those times I put ketchup in my underwear because unlike my sisters, I was ready to be grown and everyone had their cycle, but me. I was a late bloomer; I was 14. That's when it hit me. I didn't have a mother. I didn't have anyone to help me cross over into womanhood. Nobody prepared me. It made me afraid to grow up. My thoughts immediately began to race with questions. "What if I had other "mother-daughter" moments? Who would be there for me? This was getting worse and worse by the day.

I ran into my adopted mother's old room, but no one was in there except my older cousin. She had recently moved to NY to be with my mother before she died. Still searching, I dashed down the flight of stairs into the dining room then through the kitchen, down the basement stairs to my aunt's room; banging and screaming at her door, "She finally came, she finally came." My aunt quickly snapped me out of my celebration. "Who the hell came? "Aunt Flo", I said ecstatically. Without hesitation, my aunt responded, If you don't get your black a** out of my face!" I looked at the ground and somberly said, "I need a pad." She looked in her stash under the bathroom sink and threw some at me. "Here", she said, dryly shoving them in my chest, and went back to smoking a cigarette and lying in the bed. With tears streaming down my face I whimpered, "I thought it would be better than this. I'm crossing over into womanhood, I didn't even have a woman to welcome me to the other side.

My mother had skimmed over the birds and the bee's conversation with me. The only story that I remember was if you let a little boy in, you will end up like your birth mother; lots of babies and not taking care of them. So, you better not do anything with a boy until you are grown and out of my house! This put so much fear into me. I didn't want to be anything like my birth mother!

All the talk about moving had finally ended and it was official. My aunt told us we had an entire day to tell our lifelong friends that we were all moving away. I asked, "Why do we have to move? Why can't we still stay in our house?" She explained to us that our mother had gambling issues, along with unpaid bills, and other legal paperwork that prevented us from staying in the house. We were moving to South Carolina and that was that. She allowed us to pack up a few things and everything else we needed would be provided for us when we got there: a new house, a new school, and new clothes. We were moving to a brand new life.

I went to school that day to say my goodbyes. I finally met a boy I really liked and I was upset that I was going to have to leave him along with many of my other childhood friends. The entire day, my two best friends and I clung to each other. We took pictures all day. We went through four disposable cameras. Three cameras were for me and the other for them. My favorite is the picture of all of us in our homeroom class. I can't believe I had to leave my best friends, my teachers, everybody. New York was all I knew. I loved the corner stores. I would miss my beef patty with cheese and coco bread or my $.50 worth of candy. I loved the loud city buses and the fast life. Now I must trade it all for country living. I heard it was one grocery store in the whole town and the school was so much smaller.

The day of the move, we woke up at 6 a.m., packed up my mother's Cadillac and the U-Haul with our few approved items. My aunt and her sister piled us in the back seat and drove us down to South Carolina. We had our snacks, pillows, and tears. We were all sad and I was mad that I had to sit in the middle in the back for the next 12 – 14 hours. As we were pulling out of the driveway, we passed my best friend. It was 6 a.m. in the morning. She walked a few blocks at the crack of dawn to say her final goodbyes. She wouldn't miss this for the world. I watched her run behind the car with other neighborhood friends as we drove off.

Looking from the back seat, I did sign language with my best friend saying, "I will miss you and I will always love you." I also told her that I would write her every day. It was such a Color Purple moment. It would be 10 years before we would see each other again.

The ride was long and exhausting, especially because of the lack of space from being smashed in the car. We all needed to shower, so the car was also starting to smell. This seemed to go on for 14 hours. "Welcome to South Carolina", I read. We finally pulled up to a small house where it was completely dark outside; even the air was different. It all felt different as we finally got out to stretch our legs. While waiting for my aunt to come to the door, I began to look around and noticed that things were a lot cleaner down here.

We all rushed into the door, fighting to use the bathroom first. I headed to see my room, which was next to the hallway bathroom. To no surprise, my sister and I were sharing a room, again, but at least the room was nice. We had twin beds that were side by side. I peeped the closets, and they were filled with Sunday dresses. I looked in the drawers and I had everything all-new. From undergarments, new school clothes, and shoes. Whoever bought all these new clothes sure didn't ask me for my opinion, because they were all plain jane clothes. It was missing my swag, but I knew if I said anything I would probably die. I had learned to shut up from all those years of being slapped in the mouth.

After unpacking the car, I sat down on my new bed. The atmosphere was so different; I became afraid. I was hours away from what I knew to be home, but my aunt promised my adopted mother on her death bed that she would keep us all together and make sure that we graduated high school, with no kids. Life was so different without my mother. I could not find anyone to tell how I was feeling, so I just buried it all.

On the first day at the new school, we all had to meet with the principal. He took the time to give me a schedule and walk my sister and me to our classes. As I walked the hallway, I thought to myself, "Wow, everybody must be home because it's so quiet." I came from a school where it was very loud in the classroom and hallways. New York is a loud and busy city by nature, so this would definitely take some getting used to.

We arrived at the classroom, and I saw everyone staring at me as I walked in. All I wanted to do was run. Being the new kids in the school, word got around quickly that there were two new "pretty" girls from New York. Everyone was so nice, and they talked funny. After every word, there was a "yes ma'am", "no sir", or "bo"; whatever that meant. I thought it was so hilarious. I remember sitting in the classroom and the teacher called my name and I said "what". She got me straight in front of the whole classroom. She stated that I needed to know I am in the south now and if I want to be known as a respectful young lady I needed to embrace adding "ma'am" when I speak to her. It took a while, but I finally adapted. Truthfully, I didn't respect authority, so I liked to rebel. After a while, I began to make new friends and join new cliques.

While in a circle during recess, one of my friends was talking about the youth revival that was coming to our church that week. She talked about the youth from different churches throughout the entire state of SC being in attendance. She talked about the preacher that would be there and how it would be life-changing. I was so excited! I asked my aunt, and in her normal fashion, there were a lot of expletives followed up with the word NO. I was determined to go so I sent my sister in for backup. They always told her yes. My aunt finally came back and said "Be ready in 10 mins." My other aunt was coming to take us. As the service began, a lady walked out who stood about 5"0, maybe 120 pounds soaking wet. I expected a very sweet soft voice, but that wasn't it at all. The power of God fell as she moved through the room! As she began to pray, preach, and declare over people's lives, I was in awe. She moved through the crowd with power. She told us we were not too young to die and being rebellious to our parents would shorten our lives. I took these words very seriously because I was very mean, nasty, and rebellious. After preaching she called an altar call and the youth flooded the stage. I found my way through the crowd and found a chair in front of the pulpit. A lady came to me and began to pray with me and told me to call on Jesus.

As I began to call on Jesus I began to shake and cry and purge. I began to repent. I asked God to take away my lustful desires, perversion. I asked God to take the dirty dancing away. I looked around and the kids were shouting and praising. I couldn't move all I could do was speak in tongues and cry. As I stood to go back to my seat, everyone looked different. There was such a feeling of peace from that day forward. As I got home, my aunt greeted me with her common expletives. I thought to myself, man nothing changed. Although nothing changed at home, I knew something deep on the inside had changed my life and I also never danced the same again. From that day forward my relationship with God has never been the same.

I began to embrace my new home and school life because here I was, the new sheriff in town. Our house was extremely strict. It got worse after my mother died. I could not go outside. I could not have friends over. Lastly, I could not talk on the phone. It felt like I was in prison. The only thing I could do was go to school, come home, eat, clean up, and go to bed. I hated my life and I hated my home. If someone called my aunt to check on us, I would hear her talking trash about us, especially me. She would say things like, "That old ugly gal in here dumb as a doorknob. Ain't learning nothing, don't even know how to wash. I'm gone kill her if she keeps being smart."

I hated that she never had anything good to say. I knew I never wanted to be like that. Instead of being dropped off at the church doorstep, I could now ride with my aunt to church. Unknown to me, my life for the next 4 ½ years was going to be hell. My Aunt beat me for everything I did and said, just like my mother did, but hers had more power behind it. I thought she was trying to kill me because it felt like there was so much hate in her whippings.

I was the outcast in my awkward family. I mainly stayed in my room and in the bed. God forbid we went into the family room laughing too hard. Of course, I would be blamed and sent to my room. Total opposite of home, I loved when I went to school because I was the most popular and I was also the friendliest. I went all through the end of middle and high school without a boyfriend. Older guys always liked me growing up, but my aunt would threaten to hurt me if I made any of them my boyfriend. One time I had a secret valentine. He was a senior and I was a sophomore. He bought me a teddy bear with money in the roses and when I brought it home my aunt beat me for taking it and she took the money. The next day she took the bear to the principal and told the principal off telling him he shouldn't have allowed an older guy to talk to me. I was extremely embarrassed, so I just ran the guy off.

Even in my youth, I was very mature and always found myself in different groups of people listening and observing. I was great at dancing, jumping, double-dutch, and being a clown. Out of all the things I enjoyed doing, I became interested in my sophomore year of high school in JROTC and was promoted all way to Battalion Commander. The Battalion Commander is the highest rank for cadets in a battalion of over 100 cadets in high school. You get it based on your leadership ability, academic standing, and being able to exhibit the same leadership skills, on and off-campus.

I was able to get close to the commander at school. He treated me like I was his daughter. He was the first father figure I ever had in my life. He would give me life lessons. It was like he could see my future. He pushed me to have goals, set them, and achieve them. He would push my physical body to be fit and helped me to be disciplined as a leader amongst my peers. He was able to get me out of the house a few times in high school to take me on trips to different high schools to compete in battalion competitions where I would often bring the school back the title from doing drills etc. I often wonder what would have happened if my aunt would have let me participate in sports. I was competitive and often I came out on top in competitions.

He would always tell me I was going to be such a light to this world and to never lose my smile. He still checks in with me to this day! Many times, he invited me back to the high school to speak to the young cadets at the JROTC Ball annually.

My senior year I had the most superlatives for a black girl in the senior class. I had things like, "Most Likely to Brighten Your Day," "Most Flirtatious," "Prettiest Smile, and Class Clown."

Better Days Are Coming

I was not much of a dreamer, back then. I was just hoping for better days, a better family, and a better life. The transition from the big city of New York to the smallest, most country town on earth I had ever seen was one I will never forget. This small town had one of everything. There was one grocery store, one church, one red light, one police station, and one school, but your news would travel quicker than the speed of lightning. However, this town was very home-like. Everyone knows everyone and their personal business. It was a good thing that my aunt was strict. She kept people out of our business.

I wasn't going anywhere but to church and school, so I was going to be okay. I would often wonder why a town so small could speak so loudly. I forgot to mention that everyone was related to someone, somehow. I mean everyone was cousins with someone. I would always have people ask me, "Who are your people?" Once I would tell them they would say, "Oh, yeah, that's my cousin on my momma's side." I would interject and say, "I'm not really your cousin because I'm adopted. I rejected my family, just as much as they rejected me. I did not want any parts of that. I did not date anyone for this reason. Plus, my aunt was not allowing it. When we did get out for a football game, they would laugh at us and say things like, "They let us out the cave". We were very sheltered.

I had to get used to this small town. At this point, I did not have a voice in the matter; this was my home until I graduated high school. We all set our goals. I wanted to graduate, go to nursing school, and move far away from everyone. My alternative was to go into the military, preferably the Army, so I could move far, far away.

Someone may be thinking, I only had a little abuse growing up, but nothing too alarming for me to distance myself from my family, right? Wrong! I did not fit in this family that was given to me. I was the black sheep! I was different! I acted differently, looked different, and was treated differently. I was abused verbally, emotionally, and physically. I was not loved the way I should have been. I did not want to force myself on anyone that did not want me. I knew I shouldn't just accept how I was being treated. I refused to accept it and because of it, I was shunned.

Neither my mother nor my legal guardian(aunt) ever hugged me or told me they loved me. My presence was added to the budget. I was treated like I was dispensable. For example; if you do not pay your rent or mortgage, you'll be homeless, but you can find another home. As long as my body was there, so would the check be. In their mind, they could get another kid, just like they could get another house.

We never had a bond, we had a relationship like a guard in a prison cell to an inmate. She made sure I ate, had clothes but there were no emotions. Maybe this was the way she coped and was able to keep her vow to my adopted mother. I remember she kicked my older sister out when she only had 2 years of high school left because she went to beat on her and my sister fought her back. I lost my best friend when my sister left that day, but I forgave her.

Some people say I should be thankful that I didn't go without physical things because I had what I needed like food, clothes, and shelter. What they didn't know was that I suffered emotionally and mentally. Money will never be able to buy me back the mental anguish that I suffered at the hands of my mother and Aunt. I needed love, but I didn't want to be a statistic. According to reports, foster children have a high rate of prostitution, promiscuity, sex workers, sex addict, or drug addict. Also due to the lack of bonding and acceptance from a lack of parental guidance, there is no accountability in the home.

I wanted to love and to be loved. I knew I didn't want to find these things in a man, so I hid behind comedy. I became the jokester, which is a defense mechanism. I was the one that was never serious about anything. I would laugh at a funeral just to show you I was "ok". The truth is, I was not. I couldn't feel the emotions associated with love. That got me through all of my school days. I had many associates in high school, but I didn't have a real best friend. I could look at someone and could tell if they truly liked or loved me so most times, I didn't let people in. After some time went by, I finally found a true friend. He ended up being my son's father. He knew me and my thoughts and he never judged me. He gave me great advice and love.

"Everyone needs to be needed, wants to be wanted, and loves to be loved. You are human and you need to be loved just like everyone else in this world."
Anonymous

Masking

When you put on a mask, you're trying to hide something.

It can be small or big, once you put it on, typically it doesn't come right off. People don't wear masks to cover up temporarily, they are looking to become their mask. Let me break it down for you. Women love makeup. Why? Because it covers the big zits, blackheads, and any uneven skin tones, etc., right? When they wear it, they don't just wear it for a day and never put it back on. No, they wear it every day until they believe that they have no more uneven skin, all the zits are gone, and they make themselves look perfect to the outsider. They start to believe it. Until one day you see them without their mask or make-up. They are typically looking down at the ground or not making eye contact or feeling sad or down because they don't like what they see. Masking is dangerous. It makes you forget your purpose and your identity! God knew what he was doing when he created you and me. Every imperfection is what makes us unique. So, I encourage you today to remove your mask and I'll start with myself. -Diane

I learned at an early age what a mask was. My adopted mother was a strong woman. She would often share with me and my sisters that her mother died at a young age and she was left to take care of herself along with taking care of her other siblings; as young as six years old. They were poor and not able to finish grade school. A person can only give you what they have on the inside of them. I didn't realize this until later in life. When my mother nor my aunt could give me the love that I was desiring it was because they only knew how to survive! As I began to acknowledge this, I understood and I came into agreement with this revelation. I came out of agreement with what I knew to be true about my mother and aunt and I was able to forgive them both, along with my father. Once I did this, healing was waiting for me at the door. I had to forgive and I had to accept the assignment of Black Sheep Walk.

I also found out that my adopted mother's highest level of education was the fifth grade. Unfortunately, none of her siblings were able to obtain a high school diploma. My adopted mother worked for wealthy white people and because of her level of education, she cleaned apartments, hotels, and houses. She would come home after a long day and cook so we could have dinner at the dinner table. We didn't talk much which bothered me back then, but I later realized this was how she loved us; through serving and making sure we had enough to survive.

The children were not allowed to get into grown people conversations. My aunt lived with us, in the basement. She often joined us for dinner. My sisters and I ate and joked around at the dinner table. It didn't matter what was being served in my mother's house, we didn't get to waste food, or say what we didn't like. My mother didn't play any games! She would say things like, "You going to sit right there until the food is gone," or "I don't care what you don't like to eat, and "You better not let me see you waste anything!" I was a picky eater! I only liked chips and candy. My mother always told me if I kept eating all that candy, I wouldn't have any teeth went I got older. Little did they know, words have power because I lost about ten of my back teeth by the age of 21 years old.

After dinner, we had to take our baths and say a prayer before going to bed. The only time my mother asked me how my day was, was if the teacher called and told them or if I did something bad that day. I often rocked back and forth in the bed to go to sleep. My sister would keep her eyes out for me because my mother forbid me to rock in her house. She said I looked like a crazy person, but it was the only time I felt whole, at peace, and free. I didn't know then, but I was escaping from my internal pain. It was the only way I dealt with my childhood trauma and I found out later that my birth mother does this also. No one understood that I was screaming on the inside for just one hug, someone to tell me I was going to be okay, or I would become someone great. My mother was so strict that when I rode my bike around the corner if she felt like I stopped and talked to someone, she would beat me, make me come inside, and lock the bike in the shed in the backyard.

I had two best friends growing up and they would remind me of how mean my mother was and how they would be scared to live with her. My mother put such a fear of boys in my head that it made me not want to date one. If my mother saw a boy from our block in New York, she would beat me and make me put on one of my older sister's big shirts. She often reminded me of my birth mother and if I didn't stop being so fast, I would be just like her; on the streets and pregnant. My mother put unwanted fear in me. When I thought about boys, I would think that they only wanted one thing. I didn't date until I was a few months shy of graduating high school with someone that already knew for a long time. I did have a school crush, neighborhood crush, and plenty of boys who just wanted me to be theirs growing up. I did kiss a few boys in my school days while playing "Truth or Dare" or a game we called "Booty Tag". I even had a week-long boyfriend once.

He was so sweet and gentle. He bought me anything out of the candy store and would ride his bike with me from the park. One day he kissed me and landed me a brutal beating. I couldn't sit down for days. I was also stuck in my room for a few weeks.

Out of all of my sisters, I was the friendliest of us all. My oldest sister was a tomboy and because of that, she was cool with all the boys. When anyone would be interested in me, she didn't waste her time telling me because she knew what house we came from. My younger sister was a bit different. It was like we came from different homes. She still had a LOT of boyfriends and it was like she could get away with it all. It was like she was privileged or something.

She didn't come from my adopted mother, but they did adopt her when she was just shy of two years old. I could never get away with what she did. Just because she looked different from me and my sister, it was like she got better treatment and more love than I did. She wasn't a dancer, but she had a voice of an angel. All the boys liked her more than me because she was pretty with long hair. We were nothing alike. I'm not sure if my disdain for her came from the middle child syndrome or if it was because my mother gave her extra privileges. A part of my deepest pain as a child was that my mother was always taking my youngest sister's side. I often wondered if we would have a better relationship now if my mother didn't keep us apart as children. Don't get me wrong, all siblings fight and disagree, but it was like we were oil and water; we just didn't mix. The seed planted in us both was growing and separating us year by year.

I loved her but I hated the fact that my mother believed everything she said. One time she started a campfire under the dining room table and almost burned down the entire house. I was known as the "ringleader" so I was instantly blamed for it, but in reality, I was the one to put it out.

Now, I never said that I was a saint either. I did more than my fair share of dirt, but this time it wasn't me. Despite it all, I got the worst whooping that day. My mother really abused me. I screamed, "I hate ya'll", as I ran upstairs to grab my clothes, threw them in a grocery bag, and ran as fast as I could downstairs to the front door. I was running away from home. I was tired of my mother listening to everything my youngest sister said. She never took my side. Even when I told the truth, she didn't believe me. My anger grew bigger and bigger for my sister and my mother. I managed to make it to the end of the block, running as fast as I could. Looking back, I saw my sisters and cousins on my heels trying to catch me. Ahead of me was a busy road and I knew if I crossed the road, I would be homeless without a place to live because I didn't have any money. I was only twelve. I was tired and just wanted them to know that I wasn't the troublemaker. I didn't start the fire. She always took my sister's side and I was tired of it.

I decided to turn the block and make a left. My heart was racing and I was scared. My sister's kept screaming, "Diane! Diane!" As I turned around, my oldest sister had finally caught up with me. I was sweating bullets and I was terrified out of my mind. I had never tried to run away before. I was accustomed to getting beatings, but I had never ever felt this fed up. My cousin and younger sister finally caught up to me.

They were all pleading with me to return, saying, "Momma won't beat you; she just wants to talk to you." I knew it didn't sound right, but at this point, I didn't know the depth of my decision to run away. My sisters latched my arms to theirs and pulled me back to the house where my mother and aunt stood there waiting for me. I looked at both of them, scared to death. My mother said, "Girl, come in this house, I'm not going to beat you." I begged, "You sure you not," for about ten minutes.

After feeling confident enough, I stepped on the first step, and immediately my mother and aunt grabbed me and yanked me into the house. They BEAT me over and over with the blind handle and belt buckles. I attempted to reach for the phone and dialed a 9 and a 1, and then everything went black.

I woke up in my bed with a mild concussion and more dark secrets swept under my bed. My mother stood over me, asking me how I felt. "Does your head hurt", she asked. I replied, "Yes", and then tears start rolling down my face. I whimpered an apologetic, "I'm sorry for getting into more trouble." I was so tired, even at my young age, of feeling like there was supposed to be more to life or a better life. I was abused and I didn't have an outlet or anyone I could trust to tell. I was scared to tell an adult or the authorities for fear that I would be placed back in the foster care system. Life after that didn't change too much. If anything, it got worse. It was a point in my life where I didn't feel like what people saw on the outside.

I gave my life to Christ at age fourteen hoping that my life would get better at home and make me feel more complete on the inside. I had become very aggressive and rebellious. I didn't want to listen to any adults I wanted to fight all the time. My fight was because I had so many unmet childhood needs. This made it so difficult for me to become who I was meant to be!

"Unmet emotional needs during childhood causes wounds that must be healed in order for healthy relationships to be developed later in life. The pain from unmet needs affects our lives every day. Often this results in an induvial to shut down, disconnect, or even overreact."

Denise Boggs {Healing and Restoring the Heart}

Dear God, Why Me?

The day I discovered I was disowned by my family, was also the day that I realized I was truly, a black sheep. I had come home from nursing school. I had just worked half a day at McDonald's, and I was excited about my 18th birthday coming up soon. I came home to my sister gone and my aunt was not home either, which wasn't normal. I busted open my room door looking for any sign of where they may have gone. While I was looking for a note or some clue, what I found instead was a yellow piece of paper and it had a listing of apartments on it. Along with it a letter that read;

"Your checks are going to stop coming because you have now graduated high school and you need to move out. I kept my promise to your mother to get you through high school. Since your check is stopping it's time for you to go find somewhere else to live."

My heart sank to my stomach! I felt all the anger, rage, pain, disappointment, bitterness, and anguish all over again. It was like I wasn't good enough all over again. What did I do to deserve to be kicked out? I was just a child. Up until this point I hadn't really dealt with the trauma from my childhood. I hadn't even really been a grown woman yet. I was working, going to a community college and now I was being forced out in this world alone! I started blaming myself thinking I should have never started dating my son's father after high school and I should've continued on to eight years in the army like I started to. Maybe my aunt was angry with me because I chose not to sign the last and final paperwork of a more promising future to the army. I broke down and I cried in my room as I began to throw all of my clothes in a trash bag because I didn't own a suitcase. I cried until I couldn't breathe. I cried out to God, "Whyyyyyyyyy me?" I just wanted a better life for myself. I had big dreams and goals. I had a dream of being a Pediatric Nurse. My life flashed before my eyes. Would any of my dreams come true?

After throwing the clothes and shoes I wanted in a bag, I called my boyfriend and I told him what happened. "I have less than a month to get out or else I will be homeless." He replied, "WHAT!" He later told his parents, and they didn't understand. They housed two children, who were my age, and helped them with everything. They even gave them gas money.

I felt as if I didn't belong anyway, but this was just the icing on the cake. I began to call around to the places on the paper and they all said I was either too young, no credit, not enough job history, or not making enough money. I was only making $5.15

at McDonald's. Back then, that was minimum wage. I was doomed! To make things worse, my sister had the car. We were supposed to be sharing for school and work, but she fled to another state with a friend.

My aunt came home and ignored me. She went straight into her room. I followed her into her room to address the letter. Her response was, "I've put enough of my life on the back burner for y'all. "It's time I move on. Besides, me and my new boyfriend need our privacy. I told your sister she can keep the car. I'll get you a car so you can continue school and work. Now get out my face! I left her room. I went back to my room and asked my boyfriend to pick me up. The next couple of weeks flew by. It seemed as if I couldn't eat, sleep, or focus on anything.

My cell phone rang. On the other side, it was a man whose voice I didn't recognize. He advised me he was my boyfriend's father. "I'm sorry to hear about the predicament you've been put into. I have a trailer in the country that I'm renting out. I was going to gift it to my son for graduation, but since you're going through this I want to help. Can you afford $100 a month?" I cried, saying "Yes, I can." "Ok, great. I will get something in writing and then you can move in."

This was an answer from God, right? Many times, if we don't wait on God and rush to the first available option, most of the time we are operating out of flesh. When you make decisions out of emotions God isn't in it. Why? Because that same emotion you had will eventually change and whatever decision you made out of it you will have to live with it for the rest of your life. I was moving in and unpacking my clothes and my boyfriend comes in and says, "I have a surprise for you." Of course, I was eager to know what it was. He said, "I'm moving in too!" I jumped up and down and hugged him tightly. Regrettably, while hugging him, I swallowed deeply, and a feeling of regret came over me. I knew deep in my heart that God wouldn't be pleased with me.

I stopped hugging him and began walking through the new place with him. It had 2 bedrooms, 2 bathrooms, and his and her sinks in the master bedroom. It was designed for a husband and wife, which we were not. We were officially about to "shack up". This was the direct opposite of what I wanted to do, but I digressed and did it anyway hoping it would all work itself out in the end. My other aunt called while we were walking through the house and out of the blue she said, "I heard you found a place. That's good! What all do you still need?" I said, "Well, almost everything." She asked for the address and she showed up with bags a few hours later.

While she helped me put up the items, she saw my boyfriend come in with his clothes. She looked at me and said, "I know he's not moving in with you." Ashamed I said, "Yes, he is." She said, "Well, I can't help you. I was only going to help if you were doing this by yourself."

She got furious with me and left in anger, gathering a few of the things she bought me and taking them back. That really crushed me. That day, a seed of bitterness was planted. I hated the family I was adopted into. They didn't love me unconditionally. They didn't accept me when I made mistakes. I took it as they just wanted to have a reason to just not love me. It was obvious that I had to look a certain way and act a certain way to obtain their love and acceptance. I stopped talking to all of my aunts and the majority of my family for years and years. I isolated myself. All I did was work and go to school. My sister had recently had my nephew. I helped her tremendously with him. I figured if I worked and kept myself busy, I wouldn't have to deal with that pain or ever feel that level of rejection again.

A couple of years passed, and I got pregnant with a son that wasn't planned. I never had any intention of having sex nor getting pregnant. When we met, I was still a virgin, but I was vulnerable. We hadn't even been on good terms and I think I only slept with him one time that whole month, so how could this happen? As we all know, it only takes one time. The fairytale I had in my mind, that a baby could only come into this world out of two married people who were in love, proved to not be true. Was I repeating a generational cycle that I wasn't even aware of?

As the baby grew, I knew that I had to make this right. Not only was I living in sin, but I was also shunned at church for now being pregnant and not married. I was asked to sit down from all of my duties at church and I couldn't even sing in the choir anymore. I felt dirty and ashamed, so I stopped going to church. I began to put all my love and time into this guy. God is never happy nor glorified when we give all of our attention to other people and things. He may let you live in that state for a little while, even years but eventually, He will cause you to come back to Him, one way or another.

God knows how to get our attention. Especially when you're called by His name to do His will. At this point, I was succeeding in the world; taking care of our home, cooking, cleaning, and everything in between, and even staying up half of the night studying to be that nurse I dreamed about.

Never ignore that pull on your spirit, or the uneasy feeling when you are doing something that is not right in the sight of God. Most times it's called conviction. It's when the Holy Spirit is speaking to you letting you know that God has greater and more for you. God will allow us to stay in our own will for a little while. Sometimes that can mean years because He's not on the schedule that we are on. When you are called by His name, He will get your attention by any means necessary and make you uneasy about where you are so you can come out!

An Encounter with God

Have you ever had an uneasy feeling in your gut that something was about to happen? The feeling that brings fear and a knowing at the same time. The seasons had changed, and the wind was blowing leaves on the ground. I grabbed my jacket, put it on over my pink scrubs, and grabbed my keys to lock my door. While locking my trailer door, I looked up and there was a host of blackbirds in a circle around my car. I was immediately covered in fear. I unlocked the door, ran back inside, slammed the door, and bolted back into my room. I paced back and forth for minutes, which seemed like hours, thinking that I was going to be late for work.

I didn't know what was happening to me and why. I became so fearful. Unfortunately, it overwhelmed me so much that it shook me to the core. As I gathered my strength, I ran to my car and headed to work, but those same black birds seem to follow me down the road. This went on for a week. When I arrived at the hospital,l where I worked as a Medical Nursing Technician for the past few years, out of nowhere, a black cat jumped on the hood of my car. His eyes pierced mine and my heart dropped into my stomach. I yelled, "This is it! This must mean I'm dying!" I've heard stories about people who knew they were dying before they perished, so I thought this would be my moment. After seeing the black crows and black cats for a week, I knew something bad was going to happen to me. I talked to my boyfriend, at the time, and told him what I was seeing. He tried his best to ease my mind by saying it was nothing.

At the time, I was taking care of my sister's son at least 4 out of the 7 days of the week and I also had my own son. I knew that the right thing was to be married, but we were always too busy to talk about a wedding. He loved me and for the majority of the time, we were fine. We did fight sometimes and toward the end of the relationship, I started to see a different person. He was more violent than he used to be. I knew I couldn't live with a man that I wasn't married to and still expect GOD to bless me. In my opinion, a man who is serious about you knows within a few months if he wants to spend the rest of his life with you. It doesn't take years upon years!

I knew he had gotten what he wanted, which was wifely qualities, but he wasn't going to ever marry me. Deep inside, I struggled with living with my boyfriend and fornicating. I was lost. I loved GOD deep inside and I had missed going to church feeling pure and clean. Although I loved GOD and didn't drink alcohol, smoke, or party, I was still sinking in sin. I was rejected even more by my family because I wasn't married. I walked into work that morning, still fearful and terrified, trying to avoid windows and going outside for lunch. I got a call on my mobile phone stating room 316 needed graham crackers and blankets. The other technician was currently on lunch, so I gathered the items.

As I made my way into the room, there stood a young lady who was stood about 4'9', with her two-year-old son laying in the bed. As she stood by the sink washing her face, she dropped the washcloth and looked me in the face as if she had just seen a lost cousin after ten years. I said, "Good afternoon, did you call for graham crackers and a bed change?" She replied, "Just because you have a baby with him, doesn't mean you have to stay with him." As my heart began to flutter, tears filled my eyes and so many questions filled my mind.

"How does she know I'm with someone? How does she know I'm even contemplating leaving? How?" I'm a living witness, one word from a true Prophet can shift your whole life! She said, "You're the reason my son's fever won't break", with a smirk, as if she'd been waiting for me all day. I stood there, shaking with the bedding and graham crackers, still staring out the window, where I saw a black crow on the ledge. She shared how she had been in a relationship with her son's father, which was like mine, and it became evident to her that he wasn't going to marry her. She wasted 6 plus years. Chills rushed throughout my body. How could a stranger, who I've never seen before, have so much in common with me? I placed the items on the bed, gave her son the crackers, and sat down in the chair in the room as we talked for almost an hour. I was able to confide in her. The truth is, I wasn't happy in my current relationship. I had not been happy for a few years, but I thought because we had a baby together, we were supposed to stay together. These were my deepest inner thoughts. Another truth was that he was a good guy, but he also liked to drink, and he was controlling.

The relationship with my son's father had gotten so bad with all of the fighting almost every day. When I provoked him in an argument, he would hit me, often. I had a dislocated jaw one time and I remember being knocked unconscious five days after having my son. It began to get worse. When my son was five days old, we began arguing about him wanting to do something. He began to drag me from the bedroom to the living room, while pounding my head. I wanted to fight back, but I was bleeding so heavy from the stitches in my stomach that I was afraid they would burst open. So, I just laid there, and at that moment, I played dead to see if there was any love for me. I realized that the only love we shared laid there on the bed weighing in at 7lbs 22 inches long with his umbilical cord still attached, wrapped, and swaddled in a blanket. I prayed a silent prayer. "Dear GOD, if you can hear me, I'm sorry for sinning by living with a man I'm not married to, but if you can get me out of this relationship, I promise to do whatever you want me to do." I was supposed to protect him, but as I lay there, I realized at that moment that this was not God's plan for my life. I had stepped out of His will and it was going to take a lot of courage to leave this relationship. I feared being alone without a man or friend, but it pushed me to a place of being alone with God, which was what I needed. If you run from the thing God wants to deliver you from, you will find yourself right back in it. I had to go, but how do you leave what's killing you spiritually? Let God do it. I was numb. I felt like I had received a high dosage of Novocain.

He pulled me up off the floor and I looked into his eyes. He was so sad and remorseful, saying he was sorry, he didn't mean to do it. As I grabbed my aching belly, I turned away from him and looked at my less than a week-old baby laying on the bed. I scooped him up and held him close to me. I laid down and fell into a deep sleep. It was that day when my heart left the relationship. I didn't have any money or furniture, but I had decided I was leaving. It wasn't long after meeting London at the hospital that I packed my things and left completely and never looked back. London and I are still friends to this day.

Rushing to Destiny

Prophecy is a prediction or an utterance from a Prophet, inspired by God. I went into this marriage wanting my husband to be everything that was missing in my life. I wanted him to be a mother, father, lover, and friend. This was my first mistake; God should be everything we need. Also, when God gives you a prophecy, He wants you to do the work to fulfill the prophecy.

If He shows you that you will be a Doctor one day, the next day you don't go out and buy a white coat and a stethoscope and believe you're a Doctor now. You have to put in the work by completing 8-10 years of schooling, plus the clinical hours to provide "experience". Once the work is done, then you will have rightfully fulfilled the prophecy. I was young and immature, and I acted on a premature word.

While getting lunch on a gloomy, rainy day, where I stood having a late lunch in my pink scrubs, white shoes, and hair pulled in a ponytail, I was given another prophecy that would change my life. I was having a cheeseburger with fries and a coke. The cashier responded, "$6.47". As I reach for my badge to pay for my lunch, this tall black lady next to me says, "I want to talk to you." I replied, "Okay." I paid and immediately walked over to bag up my food. The lady begins speaking in the loudest, blunt tone I've heard, "That man isn't the one you will marry!" I looked up and said, "Ooookay, then who?" She said, "The man you will marry is this tall," while measuring her hand to my scalp. I thought, "Wow, that's short." My son's father is 5'10", so I knew it wasn't him. Besides, I had been free from him for about 3 months already and I was living on my own. I was taking care of my son while working and going to school.

Then she says, "He is a Prophet!" At that time, I was ignorant and didn't know what that was. She also said," He looks shy and quiet to an outsider, but he's humble." I got sarcastic with her and replied, "Well, since I'm getting a new man, what color is he?" She answered, "He's not much darker than you." Then, she had the nerve to walk off as if she didn't just turn my life, as I once knew it, upside down. At this point in my life, I was a single mother and I just wanted to be obedient to God. I didn't know what obedience would require, just like many of us, but I knew I wanted to do it His way. Sometimes, we obey God just to get out of a situation, but we don't ever stay committed to our vows long enough to see God really work in our favor.

A little part of me was afraid of being alone. I fear God, but I'm also human. I thought maybe my son's father would get saved and God would bring him back. The words that the lady spoke to me that day repeated over and over in my head. It gave me hope and raised my expectations that my obedience to God paid off. My life as I once knew it would never be the same. I felt it in my gut. My instinct told me it was God. As I walked out of the cafeteria that day, I felt joy. I looked up and there was my ex. He was a janitor in the hospital where I worked. He looked at me and I looked back at him. We didn't speak to each other; we didn't have to. At that moment, I realized I had another encounter with God. God had sent me a messenger to let me know that He had me. God would always send me someone to confirm His plans for my life.

How could I go from having a high school sweetheart, live-in boyfriend, best friend to a single mother in a matter of months? By obeying GOD! His ways are higher than ours and His thoughts are not ours. I had already begun my journey to being celibate and seeking God. I would pray all night while the Holy Spirit started to purify me inside and out as I lay in my bed alone. I heard God say to me, "Your bed is undefiled."

"Marriage is honorable in all and the bed undefiled: but whoremongers and adulterers God will judge."
Hebrews 13:4

The Holy Spirit would affirm me when I woke up in the mornings. I would affirm myself by saying things such as, "I am beautiful, I am enough, and I am a Proverbs 31 woman. I normally worked 12 – 16 hours, 3 to 4 days a week. My other time was spent in Nursing school. My son spent a lot of time with the babysitter and his grandmother. I wanted to provide a better life for him; better than the one I had for me.

I was 8 months into being single, on my own, and loving it. One weekend, I went out to eat with my two best friends at IHOP, and naturally as women do, we started talking about our love life. I said, "I'll never be in love again! I hate love, all you do is be with someone, and once they get your good stuff they leave." I had not yet realized that all men aren't the same.

This type of thinking was proof that I needed deep healing. There were deep wounds I had not yet dealt with so that I could heal from the past. When I didn't get my way in relationships or we had disagreements, I would be quick to call whoever I was dating out of his name or provoke a fight because deep down inside a part of me only knew how to sabotage. I would damage a good thing because as I knew my life up to now, no one stayed in my life anyway. There was so much healing that the little girl inside of me needed.

The spirit of self-sabotage causes destruction, death, and devastation. It focuses on the insecurities of the individual to destroy personal progress or ground gained. Sabotage is sent to stop, hinder, and discourage opportunities of growth and stop God's appointed destinies, purposes, potentials, dreams, visions, and relationships. The agenda is to stop and deliberately prevent the operation of success.

The best way to identify this spirit is if you are holding on to unforgiveness, pride, jealousy, a lying tongue, a controlling spirit, or anger, you may be dealing with self-sabotage. Begin to uproot the spirits of rejection, unforgiveness, lying, and the Python spirit. I decree and declare with you that God will uproot the spirit of self-sabotage out of you, and you will begin to live a life of freedom to believe in the promises of God, and not reject His plan for your life. Always remember that rushing into destiny will leave you in a traffic jam!

Problem or Prophecy?

"Psalm 34 reads, "I will bless the Lord at all times. His praises shall continually be in my mouth." I was sitting in the choir at our annual Sunday school Convention reading along with the Pastor, when I heard a whisper in my ear say, "There he goes." I looked up, and it was the parents of a guy I had known since I was just fourteen years old. I waved and they waved back. "Wow, I haven't seen their son in at least five years or so," I thought to myself.

As we took our seats on the choir stand, in the back door comes the guy I was just thinking about. We instantly locked eyes and smiled and waved at each other. He was short, quiet, and looked very peculiar to the outsider. It was like something inside of me was jumping for joy. Every time I looked up he was looking me in my eyes. For the first time in a long time, I couldn't tell you what the preacher spoke about because I was so invested in him.

When church was over, I made my way to the back door and went around to greet him. We hugged and his eyes pierced my soul as if he had known me my whole life. After church ended, a mutual friend who texted me 10 min later saying he wanted my number. I'm thinking, "Why couldn't he just ask me? I was right there in his face. I texted him my number and we talked on the phone the first day for 9 hours straight. It was so supernatural. I connected with him on a level that I never felt before. I'll never forget, he said, "Do you feel that?" It was like a rushing of energy that consumed me. It felt like euphoria. I felt like I was floating on clouds. He knew me, I knew him, we shared so many similarities. My life was lining up with his. He had recently gotten out of a relationship and so did I. He said the reason why he was staring at me on the choir was because he said I was glowing like an angel with a halo. He had never seen that before on anyone. I didn't have to be someone else around him. He knew early on what was important to me. He knew that I had a calling on my life, and I was called to be a preacher. He said he was too. He knew my story and he accepted me. He knew my deepest secrets and didn't judge me. I knew his and I accepted him.

Everything with us moved quickly. Mainly, because I felt like he was "the one". It is just a feeling you have when you've found "the one"! There aren't many words to explain the chemistry or the connection. My days consisted of working and even while at work I couldn't get enough of him. We had become each other's worlds; inseparable.

After a few months of talking on the phone all day and sleeping on the phone at night, he started to come over to my apartment. My years of celibacy all came to an end with one kiss. I know James 4:7 reminds us to resist the devil and he will flee, but the truth is that I didn't want to resist it. I wanted what I thought was mine. We couldn't resist each other for several hours straight. I had fallen into temptation and I found myself begging God to forgive me and falling right back into the sin of fornication.

Thinking to myself, "Didn't God just deliver me out of this already? How did I end back up here again?" The truest answer is that I persuaded myself that because I was going to marry him, he was different. God's word wasn't different. We just altered it to fit what we wanted. My Godmother told me what most Christian singles are told, "It is better to marry than to burn."

The truth of the matter is that I didn't wait until God purified us. He wanted me and I wanted him. We justified our actions because we had known each other since we were both fourteen, on the state youth choir, and we thought we had known each other for life.

After that night, we were married within six months. We thought we knew each other based on the number of years we had known each other. I was so determined to make the prophecy come to pass that I didn't check with God. I took him at face value. I didn't know this man at all, and I paid a very high price of regret, almost losing my life, having his babies, and a lifetime of scars, just for rushing into it.

He was everything I needed. He was loving. He was a good listener. He pleased me sexually. He had it all together, kind of sort of. He had the charm, the wit, the words, he was a great listener, very intelligent. He graduated as a high school salutatorian. He had countless awards. He put his family through school. He was a top-notch guy. I thought I had hit the lottery! I thought with his mind and my love we would be the perfect couple; unstoppable. He knew what to say and how to say it. He made me feel like all we needed was more time and we would have everything God promised us.

His only problems were that he smoked weed and he didn't want to go to work. Of course, as I addressed it, he said he would stop smoking and go find a job. Simple as that. I believed him. If he told me the sky was purple, I believed him because he was my ordained mate. There was nothing we could not overcome.

The first few months were perfect. We had a baby girl our first year of marriage! Four years later we had another baby girl! We were in honeymoon bliss. Then, hell opened up; his mask fell off. He wasn't who I thought he was. He flipped back and forth between personalities, but I loved him. What I came to realize was that he was a master manipulator. He said all of the right things to make me feel like he was changing, but he never really changed. Years went by and he promised to stop smoking and to turn his life around to serve God, but it never happened. I would often ask him, "What is the vision for our marriage?" He would reply, "Get this money and get rich. That's it." Knowing I was seeing more for our life spiritually than he was, I often questioned myself. "Did I make the right decision in this marriage because we were growing apart?"

I wanted a husband. I wanted to be accepted. I wanted to be provided for and protected. However, he wasn't a provider, I was. He didn't have a job for 5 years, nor the drive to make anything happen. I mean, he did bring in a little money from time to time but nothing consistent. He was employed through different "under the table" jobs like family and church, but nothing consistent. Even though he wasn't working, I thought it would be ok. I felt like my love would pay for it all. He wasn't a protector, I was. I never felt safe. Isn't a husband supposed to be those things? I thought the potential was enough to fulfill the prophecy because I wanted a happy ending. He did just enough to get me and then once we were a couple, he changed. He became very controlling, making me feel like I wasn't worth anything. He told me I was fat. If my teeth were whiter, I would be prettier. If I had surgery, I would be skinnier. I was never enough. I believed him. My friends left. My family wasn't coming around anymore. I lost my job. The car I had paid off, I lost.

Be careful of people who come into your life portraying to be one way and as a result, you end up losing everything. Any relationship, be it intimate or just a friendship, love should be reciprocal. It should be a two-way street. I found myself being the man and woman in my marriage. It was not balanced. I did all the wifely duties and everything he should have done. It caused me to be overworked and overwhelmed. I suppressed a lot of my emotions because I didn't want to lose him.

"Nothing destroys self-worth, self-acceptance, and self-love faster than denying what you feel. Without feelings, you would not know where you are in life. Nor would you know what areas you need to work on. Honor your feelings. Allow yourself to feel them!"

-Iynalya Vanzant

I had seen some of the lowest days of my life. At this point in my life, it was filled with so many disappointments that it made my heart ache, literally. My daily activities, like taking a shower, eating, taking care of my children, working, being a wife, and even walking all came to a screeching halt on January 9, 2013. As I laid in the hospital bed with E.K.G wires on my chest, legs, and head, along with IV drips and oxygen, I reflected on the undue stress that I was under just trying to hold it all together. I had doctors pacing in and out of my room, and nurses in and out, all looking at me with fear in their eyes.

One of the nurses looked at me and mouthed these words to me, "You are gonna be just fine!" Looking to my right my husband was laying in the bed with me, and our fresh new infant was in her car seat. My son stood by the sink in fear as he looked at me not knowing what landed me in the E.R that afternoon. He was terrified wondering what was happening to his mommy. I looked at the monitor. My heart rate was close to two hundred! My blood pressure was dropping lower by the minute. I felt closer to death than life. I was afraid to die. That has always been one of my biggest fears. Not just to die, but to die young and not accomplish anything in life.

I prayed, "God please help me, don't let me die young. My family needs me." Shortly after my prayer, a Cardiovascular

Doctor came in and he scratched his head. He asked if I had any family history of heart problems? I could barely talk because I was so short of breath. I shook my head no and said, "I'm adopted. I don't know my real family history." He replied, "Ma'am your heart is enlarged, and it looks as if you have Postpartum Cardio-Myopathy. It is a rare type of heart failure. It occurs during pregnancy or immediately after delivery. The conditions weaken the heart muscle and causes the heart to become enlarged. As a result, the heart can't pump blood properly to the rest of the body."

According to the American Heart Association, this heart condition affects 1,000 to 1,300 women in the United States each year. Women usually receive a diagnosis during the last month of their pregnancy or within five months of delivery. Cardiomyopathy can affect your health for the rest of your life. Even after successful treatment, the treatments include heart transplants, beta-blockers, diuretics, and drugs that strengthen the heart to improve pumping and circulation.

He continued on asking, "How many children do you have?" I replied by holding up two fingers. He said, "Well that's good." "Thank God because I wouldn't recommend you have any more. The next one may kill you!" He walked out of the room. I turned to my husband with tears in my eyes. I began crying saying, "I told you something was wrong." I started to blame him for my diagnosis. I needed to blame anyone but myself.

I started to think back to when I was only two weeks postpartum. I remember showing off in the house doing all the housework, vacuuming, and wearing my little tight dresses with high heels giving my hubby something to look at. I remember breastfeeding the baby and not eating or drinking but once or twice a day. This is surely what did it right? I mean I was only 25 with seemed like a death sentence. I was so devastated, but I wiped my tears like I always did and allowed the doctors who I trusted to take care of me and fix me.

I was admitted into the ICU on the cardiac floor. I was quickly told, "You are the youngest patient on this whole floor," with fear in their eyes. The next week was spent alone, no hubby or kids. I remember the Doctors coming in asking if I had any support? I proudly said, "Yes of course." Some would have a look of concern. One even replied, "Well this is the time for them to be here with you!"

Often, children that were raised as orphans or alone tend to think being alone is normal, but in reality, it's called dysfunctional thinking. I was laying in the ICU with no one I could talk to or cry to; that wasn't normal!

My next visitor was no shock to me. It was my former Pastor. He was such a prayer warrior. If any sick was among any of his leaders, he made sure he prayed for them! While he was praying for me he said, "Baby, the Lord is trying to get your attention. You have a calling on your life." I've heard of people running from God and what he wanted them to do but I didn't think of myself from running from God. I had gotten out of my fornication and now I was married and I was back in church. That was enough, right? Wrong. He was right! I was running from my problems and I had mastered being religious. I went to church on Sundays, wore my long skirts, and looked like I was holy to the outsider. I lost my faith in who Jesus really was. I only trusted what I could see. I had so much pain and trauma from my past that I never really dealt with.

While I was in the hospital, I had a lot of time to sit with God and my thoughts. God even showed me having problems with men. The real reason behind me only having been in two relationships with men was for one major reason. I was taken advantage of by girls growing up. I would have flashbacks of being made to hump girls my age when I was around 7-10. It all started with my friend from the church. Some days my mom would be late picking us up because she was at Bingo, so we would have to walk home. She was the girl next door. She said we were gonna play "house", but she began to touch me in my private areas. She allowed her teenage brother to watch. We were only 7 at the time. This went on for about 5 years. I remember this even followed me in middle school. I liked it at one point, but deep down inside I knew it was wrong. I had perversion on the inside of me and no one ever dealt with it from the root. Boys rejected me mostly in my youth because I was very skinny with no butt or chest. I was a late bloomer. I was never attracted to girls, but I could never say no to what they wanted me to do to them. I had secrets and God knew them all. I took the little Bible he gave me to read and I thought, "Why does God want to use me? I'm not good. I don't have anything to tell anyone." Over the next few years, it seemed like pure torture. They were some of the worst days and nights of my life, as I knew it then.

As I ended my stay at the hospital, I was sent home to take beta-blockers. I stopped taking them less than a month on them. I started to have symptoms of having a stroke and my legs would twitch and burn all night. It felt as if I was running miles in my sleep.

As a result, my heart would race and wake me up in my sleep. It felt like I was dying all over again. Every. Single. Night. I would wake up and reach over to my hubby to help me and he would just say I was okay, and turn over. Sometimes if I screamed loud enough, he would wake up and get me cold water to throw on my legs, which seemed like the only thing to calm the nerve down and my heart rate. I was scared for my life. This couldn't be God's will. I couldn't make love to my husband for almost a year. I felt like I was dying if I did. He became more distant from me. He was supposed to love me through sickness and health, right? I felt so alone. Everything around me looked and became so dark. I didn't want to eat, I lost so much weight. I remember falling out of bed one night during an attack and I said, "God if you get me out of this, "I will do your will! YES, Lord, I submit. Please take this away." I heard God say to me, "Whatever your hands find to do, you must do it with all thy heart and with all thy might"! I said, "Okay, God."

God wanted me to trust Him and have faith and I wasn't quite there yet. When I had an attack with my heart rate, I would call 911, the ambulance would come and take me to the hospital. After about twenty trips, I will never forget when the EMS came in nonchalantly and proceeded to ask my husband about the video game he was playing, instead of attending to me, the patient. They asked if I had anxiety, I said, "I don't think so." My hubby, who at this point ignored all my attacks, turned around with aggravation in his voice and screamed, "Yes!" They took me in and this African American cardiologist came in and said, "Wow, you're really young ma'am." I said in my most pitiful voice, "I know. Can you help me?" He said, "I will try my best. I'm going to run some tests and see if I can help you!" As he was doing an ultrasound on my kidneys, my heart rate suddenly dropped to 44. He said, "Are you okay?" I said, "I think so. I just feel weird." I think you are still healing from having a new baby", he informed me. He began to go into a story about his wife not healing until after a year. At that moment, I heard a small still voice that said, "They won't ever find what's wrong with you! Don't put your faith and trust in man they will fail you! Trust me." That was the last day I went to the hospital for those attacks! God has a way to help us to trust him wholeheartedly. I stayed with my affliction longer than I probably could've if only I would've trusted God sooner!

I'll never forget while on my face in prayer, I heard God tell me I had healing power in my right hand. It wasn't until four years later that I used these hands to lay hands on my aunt's best friend. I told her that I could see her laying in a bed and God said, "Go lay hands on her feet and pray to me to heal her." As I prayed, the Doctors were coming in giving bad news to the family saying she had no brain activity after she had a heart attack. They said she went without oxygen too long, but I didn't let that stop me from praying. I kept on praying that if God raised me up out of my sick bed, He surely could do it for her! The woman recovered after long rehabilitation and she was able to return home to her husband and young child.

All God wants is for us to believe Him, trust that whatever we are needing Him to do for us He can and will do it! If I had not believed God could heal me from this death sentence, I would've been a young, disabled, depressed, young girl. I even contemplated suicide while in this mental state. But GOD!

God is the healer, deliverer, and way maker! He oftentimes puts us in situations that seem impossible so He can get the glory from it. Without a doubt, God gets ALL the glory from my life. I don't know where I would be if He hadn't had these special moments and encounters to invade my life showing Himself great and mighty! I no longer have Cardiomyopathy. They even went back to look just to make sure. I am free from it all. When you submit to God, He will wipe all of your afflictions away. He told me on my sickbed;

"You shall not die, but live and declare the works of the Lord. The Lord hath chastened me sore, but He has not given me over unto death."
Psalm 118:17-18

Nine years into the marriage, I finally accepted the fact that I married wrong. I was tired. I was back on my face, crying, and praying to God, feeling like a failure as a wife. Ultimately, I felt like a failure of what God honors; marriage I realized I had made lots of mistakes in my marriage and one of them was putting too much expectation on my husband to be everything I needed and wanted him to be. I married him when he didn't have a job, just to prove my love for him. Just to prove I would support him no matter what. I did it just to prove that I would be there for him when no other woman would take him. First mistake of many.

I learned that you don't have to prove anything to anyone on this earth. If it's real, the world will KNOW it, and you will know it as well. I didn't care about the name-calling, the isolation, the unemployment, or smoking weed, but what hurt the most was when I was on my death bed, he didn't care. How could I have married someone who didn't care about my well-being? God took me back to the root of the issue when was when I was on my sickbed. My husband wasn't compassionate.

When I couldn't perform for my husband in bed, he looked outside our home for fulfillment. It gave so much room for the enemy to come in.

He disrespected me and on top of it, he wasn't attracted to me anymore and he let me know it. We fought more than we loved each other. I wanted to fight FOR my marriage, but not IN my marriage. We went to see about 4 different marriage counselors, but none of them could help. Not because they were not great counselors, but because he wasn't willing to do the work to produce change.

I was vulnerable when I got married. I wanted so much from him, so to please me he became what I needed. I never checked back in with God. When his non-compassionate side showed up, I was blindsided. I didn't know him like I thought I did. Thinking back to when we got married, he only knew me from church and at that time, my skills in the bedroom. That is not knowing someone's true soul or character. Marriage is when two people become one in their mind, will, and emotions. Becoming one is a give and give; yin and yang. Where one is weak the other can be strong. We attempted to master some of this, but not all. He was a great man, indeed. However, He was just as broken as I was. He needed God's love to heal him just as much as I did. He rejected God and I could no longer help him. Trying to fix him, broke me. Most of the time, women who are lovers and healers find themselves attracting broken men. Remember, there is only one healer; the Great I AM.

Our marriage was absolute heaven until he took me through hell. We got married really young. I suffered all nine years of my marriage because we both had the love of God, but we didn't honor Him in our ways. We both abused each other verbally, emotionally, and physically.

A month into the marriage he threw me into the wall and then choked me. He began to hit me and I began fighting him back. He said he would never hit me and I believed him. Of course, he knew everything I had gone through as a child, teenager, and young adult, so I expected him to be different. But it wasn't. I never saw him this aggressive. We fought for 6 years. I was over it. I was so disappointed that my kids had to watch me fight the man I loved, their father. He cursed me out in front of them. I remember calling my in-laws and they encouraged me to stay. "This happens all the time." "All marriages go through this." I was disgusted that Christians would give this kind of advice. It was not long after that I found out this was normal back in the day. It might be normal for somebody, but I was determined that I was getting out.

We came in with a lot of baggage from our childhood and our past in general. A lot of the seeds that were planted in me as a little girl had now fully grown and I only could speak from the hurt that was deep down inside of me. As the old saying goes, "What's in a person is also what comes out of a person." For so long, my testimony was that I had only slept with my son's father and my husband. I wore this as a badge of honor as if I thought I was better because I had fewer partners.

I was angry with my husband because he left me when I needed him the most. I had gotten so bitter and angry in my marriage until I fell into adultery as well. I cheated back out of anger and many unmet needs. When it all started it was just as a thought of being with someone better. I wanted a man who loved God and had a nice body. I would dream of this man almost every night, until one day I looked up and he was there standing right in front of me. I heard the small voice telling me to stop thinking about him, but I kept ignoring it. Eventually, I had thought about it so much I manifested it into my life.

In an attempt to reconcile, I returned to my marriage. We were separated for a while to work on ourselves. When I returned, I gave it my all, the cheating had stopped on my behalf. I became consistent in my prayer life, returned to the church, and started back doing all of the wifely duties. I didn't look at him to change. He continued to do what he had been doing all of these years. I caught him cheating via snap chat. I found multiple text messages. To make matters worse, it was all on my birthday. He continuously put his hands on me, belittled me, and never covered me in prayer. He did get around to getting a great job and could provide for me financially, but I finally realized I wasn't HAPPY! I deserved to be happy and so did he. I think he was just as done as I was. We just didn't know how to let each other go. I didn't want another prophecy or another person to tell me to stick it out!

I didn't ever have anyone tell me I deserved better, but I finally decided to stand in the mirror and tell myself. I deserved better. Dysfunction was my norm from childhood, so how was I supposed to know? The spirit of God in me finally started to show me the truth and I finally started to listen. I knew I deserved a king that would honor me, knew how to protect me in the natural and spiritual, buy me nice things, celebrate our anniversary, heck, even buy me a wedding ring! No, we didn't even have those. I wanted a best friend that would laugh at all my corny jokes and I would laugh at theirs. God showed me, that before the foundations of the world, I was created to be a Proverbs 31 woman. He created me to love. He sent me to speak with wisdom. I am a God-fearing woman. I am a nurturer who loves to take care of my home and my children.

However, I didn't feel like any of that was true. In reality, I felt more like the dirt on the ground. I often felt walked on, like a doormat. I had invested so much into it. After almost losing my life after giving birth to our girls, I was exhausted and I needed answers. I tried to fix everything my way. That didn't work.

I finally decided to come to Jesus broken, I didn't know what else to do. As I labored in prayer for hours, day after day, and month after month, I felt led to go to another church. At the end of the service, the Pastor prophesied to me by saying, "Your next move is the right move! You know, the one you've been thinking about?" She expounded and said if I am obedient to God, He will bless me with my heart's desires. I knew God had answered my prayer just as he did with Hannah in the Bible. She came to God with a broken spirit and He answered her by filling her belly with promise! Jesus cannot come down in the flesh anymore, so instead, He will use different messengers to get His word to you. Sometimes, He uses the Prophets, nature, children, road signs, or whatever He has to, to speak to you. In biblical times, He even used a donkey.

Familiar spirits are real. They come to keep us stagnant and never reach our destiny or full potential. All we have to do is stay in God's presence, stay in his will, and He will send them. God had let me know that I married wrong, and although He graced me to live through it all these years, it wasn't His ultimate plan for me. God has an ordained mate just for me. The one that He promised me before I fell in love with who I was now only familiar with.

I am now divorced and I am not upset about it. I am happy that I chose myself and my happiness. After all the hell I've been through, the least I deserve is true happiness. My ex-husband and I are great co-parents to our children. He respects my journey and I respect his! I pray that God blesses him in this lifetime to also find true happiness. He is one of the GREATEST fathers to our children.

It is okay to admit if a relationship doesn't serve you anymore. Sometimes you grow apart. The closer I got to God and began to heal from all of my childhood trauma, lust, and perversion, the more we grew apart. Sometimes, people are only attracted to the part of you that is broken. There is another group of people that are waiting on the whole, healed, renewed version of you. I was finally able to say goodbye to the broken little girl who wanted everything that no one ever gave her. I am a whole woman in pursuit of everything MY God promised me and just like King David, I shall recover it all! In the end, he was not my promise. The problems we endured led me to my healing, and for that I am grateful. The prophecy is still waiting to be fulfilled. Stay tuned, because God's word never comes back void!

Mom? Is That You?

It was around 4:00 am and I couldn't sleep that night from heartburn. I got a message from a woman on my Facebook messenger; *I think I am your birth mother.*

As I read those words, my stomach began to turn, and my heart began to beat really fast. Here I am, a few months pregnant with my second child. As tears stream down my face, I began to read her words to me. She began to tell me where my birthmark is and my birthdate; also known as the day she left me in the hospital. I knew she was my mother. My intuition started sending me all the signals. I clicked on her profile picture and I began to see similarities in myself that I knew she was my mother. We talked back and forth in messenger for a while until I finally couldn't take it anymore. I asked her, "Can you call me?"

I gave her my number and five minutes later she called. So here she was, after twenty-five long years. As the phone rang, I was so nervous. I answered, but I didn't even say hello. I put my phone on mute. "Hello, Diana?" I remember hearing her raspy voice, kind of like a smoker. I didn't let her hear the tremble in my voice. I kept her on mute while she talked. Her next words made my heart rejoice, "I'm clean for 9 years from the drug addiction. I'm free. God freed me." She never said she was sorry, but it was the best apology a girl like me, could ever hear. Yes, I was a grown woman on the outside, but the little girl inside of me finally got to talk to her mother. Even though she didn't say she was sorry, "I replied, "I forgive you!" I didn't have any hate inside or anger at the moment, I just felt like God was blessing me.

Talking with her over the phone, this was one of the first yet blunt conversations I had with my biological mother as I laid on the couch rubbing my five-month-old pregnant belly. She said, "Diana, I will never forget carrying you. I was pregnant every 9 months. I tried to hide this pregnancy. You know, with big shirts and stuff. Your father didn't suspect anything because we were still snorting and getting high together. Somehow, he found out I was pregnant with you. Out of all my pregnancies, I will never forget this one, because he tried to kill you! We started fighting and he pulled out a knife and stabbed me everywhere, even in my belly. I was rushed to the hospital and that's when you were born and left you in the NICU!"

As she told me her account of this story, I sat there, numb. Stunned. I had so many questions, yet I now had so many answers.

After talking days and days, it turned into a couple of years. I found out so much about my family roots. My grandfather died in the military in his early thirties and my grandmother had multiple sclerosis and she couldn't take care of all of her children so she gave them all away. My mother was in foster care at the age of five. She ran away at nine and the streets got a hold of her. Her sister, my aunt, hustled to make sure it never happened to her child. The cycle did skip him but then he had a child who is now being raised by my aunt. My mother's siblings were displaced in foster care and to my aunt and mother's knowledge, they have heard from them a few times. A few of my sibling's children are raised by different people.

There was no doubt about it, we have a generational cycle here of abandonment which leads to dealing with the spirit of rejection. Sometimes the person sent to break the cycle is not the one that is often praised or worshiped. Most times the person breaking it doesn't even know they are, they just know everything they ever want in life wasn't easy. Because of this, the hunger grows inside of them to never give up and won't let them give up. It leads to getting everything they want in life.

Even if that means they celebrate themselves or if no one ever cheers them on, they know they have to fight and continue until there is nothing left to fight for! I'm grateful to have been able to birth my three children and bring them home from the hospital and raise them. I'm grateful that I'm overcoming the rejection of being abandoned and living my life without a mother's touch. You know the touch? The one that bonds a mother and a daughter for life?

She sent me packages for me and my daughter. I'll never forget my first package from her. It was around my birthday. It was a huge brown box. It had about twenty dresses in there. She was trying to give me one for every birthday she missed. I didn't even want to wear them. I just held them all and tried to let the idea of actually having my birth mother in my life sink in. I don't have to wear the label of a motherless child. I don't have to resent the fact that my adopted mother is now deceased. I don't have to walk around in this world trying to fit in. God gave me reconciliation with my own mother, who I kind of look like, sound like, and we definitely have the same fashion style. My husband was so happy for me. Actually, everyone I told was. To top it off, I reunited back with my baby sister, brother, and my mom's sister. After talking for two years, we decided to have our first family reunion.

The day had finally arrived. My family was driving fourteen hours from up north. I even bought a new outfit for the occasion. As I sat in the beautician's chair, my heart was pounding so fast. She was late coming down. I got word that she was still trying to find something to wear. Finally, there she was. She stood about 5'9. She had on an all-white dress with pink and silver jewelry that draped over her hands and fingers. She was beautiful and perfect to me. I noticed one of her eyes was almost shut, which I later learned that she is legally blind in one eye, due to diabetes. She later showed me many stab wounds on her hands, wrist, and belly, which she said came from my father, along with many of the men that tried to kill her.

She had battle wounds, as did I. Some could be seen, some could not. She smiled and hugged me. She grabbed my hand to hold as I guided her through the hotel, to the van, as we went to go get food. The weekend was so surreal. Even though we didn't know how to communicate with each other and there were many behind-the-scenes arguments and disagreements amongst the adults, I didn't care. I just looked around me, grateful to God thinking, "Wow, this is all my family and I'm so grateful." I was walking in euphoria all weekend. I felt like I was floating on a cloud.

That Sunday, I met more of my family from a local town near where I lived. I never knew my real great-grandmother lived not far from where I lived. It was only 15 mins away. She lived until she was 101 years old. I saw a picture of her and she looked like she was so fierce! She also looked like she was a praying woman! I didn't want them to leave, but I knew the time had come for them to go. We all gave hugs and somehow we managed to not cry. That's one thing I also noticed about my family. We didn't cry all weekend. We just smiled and laughed and we all hid behind the mask.

I helped my mother onto the passenger's side of the van. I noticed that she started to look at me differently. She didn't smile at me as much as she had been and she kept walking away from me. As I shut the door, I went to my car. I didn't know when we would all see each other again, but I was hopeful. As I got home I was exhausted. My phone dinged and as I reached for my phone I looked down and the text read, "You were not who I wanted."

All I read was rejection, rejection, rejection. My heart fell to the floor. I deleted the whole message and I fell to the floor crying. How could this happen, AGAIN?" I screamed. I was furious, hurt, and I had nothing to say. I didn't want to talk to anyone. I did what I knew how to do. I ran away from my problem, pain, and the pressure of it all.

The fantasy family reunion just crumbled before my very eyes. I lived five minutes away from all of my adopted family, and they didn't come to see me nor did I see them. I now don't have a relationship with my birth mom, not to mention my marriage was hanging on by a tiny thread. I had reached my breaking point.

I did try to rekindle the relationship, but she continued to let me know I wasn't enough. She wanted to convince me to let her tell her story, but for me not to tell mine. She said I had nothing to be sad about, she was the one with the hard life. She left me in safety at the hospital, and that was supposed to be good enough. It was at that moment, that I realized I had enough healing to set myself free and to continue the journey to break the curse. My new reality; sometimes you have to be the curse to break the curse. I forgave my mother that day. I want to let you know on your journey to healing and remaining free that it will require you to also remain strong.

As I listened to my mother on the other line, I realized it was hard for her to accept my growth, my heart, and my ability to forgive. I loved her even deeper at that moment, but I also understood God had given me enough strength to cut the cord. I had submitted my whole heart to God and I have an assignment to complete on this earth. God allowed me to get what I needed from my mother and he healed my heart enough to see her as well as the bloodline. Now I know why I am needed to break the cycle. I realized I was not her. My assignment was different than hers. Although she birthed me into this world, I was sent by God to break a generational cycle that had plagued my bloodline for more than 3 generations. I didn't need anyone's permission to walk into my God-given assignment, not even hers.

Motherless Child

Who am I? Who's am I? Who do I see? Who do You see?

I have questions, God! I have answers, He replied.

I'm a helpless newborn that was left in a nursery for 27yrs waiting to be brought to my mommy.

So, she can feed me from her bosom of wisdom I've been starving for her touch.

You know the touch.

The one that bonds a mother to a daughter for life.

Hoping she can pass me her baton of intuition, Mothers that is.

But instead, I got shipped off to the next available bed.

I mean home.

I mean shelter where I laid helpless, hoping that she just forgot about me and my seven siblings.

A cold dark room where my heart began to rot from loneliness and now bitterness and anger.

Wait! Don't touch me! I'm only three!

If home is where the heart is, I don't have one!

One. One. One.

You can hear a ton of echoes where my heart used to be.

A dark hollow shell is what I see. I'm withering away you see.

I know who I am.

I'm a motherless child who's been lied to, abused mentally, emotionally, and physically.

Physically I'm appealing, but I don't think so because my mother never told me.

But wait! Why am I looking for her to validate my love?

All she ever gave me was false hope, bitterness, loneliness, and anger.

My love came from God.

It was He who sent his only begotten son to die so that I may live and love again.

I command you, motherless child, to love again.

Love your daughter the way that God loves you so that she can live.

Mother...but I can't feel her she's...but God, I don't wanna love her, because she left me.

She didn't care when she was getting high selling her body for a dollar to repeat her cycle of love.

She chose drugs and money over the precious life you gave her, so she didn't cherish what you gave to her, so I won't cherish her.

But daughter your job is not to love her the way she loved you, but to love her the way I love you.

I'm patient with you, I give you joy for today and forevermore.

I'm forgiving of you for your countless sins.

Forgive her.

But the pain won't let me. It hurts.

Ironically, even though she doesn't love me, I love her.

I love her because she taught me what love is not.

Love is not selfish.

It's not loneliness, it's not pain, it's not molestation, it's not abuse, emptiness, confusion.

It's not all the things that eat away from love.

It should not be a disease like cancer.

It should not produce seeds like hate and bitterness and offense and desperation.

But it should produce peace, calmness, joy, laughter, togetherness, and oneness with you God.

Daughter, I command you to let down the wall of offense and let forgiveness move in.

Although the memories will always remain, my daughter, let me remove the pain.

The battle is not yours it's mine.

Removing the Mask

Many people don't know they are wearing masks because it truly becomes a part of their DNA. Masking becomes a part of your blueprint. It can also travel from one generation to the next. If you have children, at different times of your life, you will see them deal with the things you have dealt with in your life. The reason why it is generational is because it remains unidentified or unconquered from one generation to the next. Someone may know that the curse exists, but who will be bold enough to stop it from going to the next generation?

I remember praying for God to elevate me about 4 years ago. Immediately, God took me into an open vision where He showed me myself. Yes, God began to show me that I was rejecting who He was calling me to be. He showed me elevating, but He also showed me if I didn't deal with this stuff at a lower level, it would be elevated with me. That's why you see Preachers who have problems. Their gift didn't stop just because they refused to deal with their issues. The gift comes without repentance, but the true anointing comes with a consecrated lifestyle and dealing with your past. It ultimately still causes them problems in the long run.

I also saw that I had buried a lot of things that were hidden such as anger, lies, lust, bitterness, and a few other things. Of course, like many of us do, we ask God to get it out of us. Well, little did I know, over the next 4 years of my life, as I knew it, would not be as I've always lived. Things began going downhill fast.

I started having a secret relationship with a guy because my marriage was in shambles. I didn't really want to go to church anymore. I got so deep in my mess that I just wanted out! I needed answers so I started telling everyone around me my personal issues, as if they could help me. It didn't matter if I knew you or not, I wanted everyone to know my business and my life status. One of my biggest mistakes was trusting people instead of going to God. I ran from my heart issues. I thought if I stayed busy, they would disappear.

In all of my searching, I had gotten extremely close to my husband's aunt. She became like a mother to me. When I met her, she said, "God told me to prepare my home for you." At that time, I didn't know who I was in God, so I didn't take those words seriously. I stayed with her for about a month as I settled in my new city of Greenville, SC. She took me to church with her the first weekend I came. As I sat on the last chair of the church, a preacher laying hands on individuals and speaking into their lives.

My aunt suggested that I get in the line to get prayer. I hesitated, but I got in the line. It seemed like she prayed for everyone in the church until she was sweating and exhausted. I sat back in my seat and observed. My aunt stared at me and told me to get back in the prayer line. I listened, but the way the lady looked, I didn't think she would have time for me. She looked too tired to pray for me because over half of the church was already slain in the spirit on the floor.

I felt like I was just standing there looking crazy and she looked at me and said, "You're a Prophet!" I looked behind me like, "Who me?" She said, "Yes you!" There was something on the inside of me that leaped and jumped. Something inside of me connected with her and knew what she just spoke was the TRUTH! I went back and sat down and my aunt's husband looked at me and said, "I KNEW IT! God told me who you were."

My life, as I knew it, has never been the same. I looked over at my aunt and she was still leaping up and down with joy and excitement because she already knew this and was now happy that I knew. The truth is, I really didn't know a lot, but if this would explain why I had to go through so much as a child and in life, I'll take it. It's like getting rewarded for your trouble. At that moment, I felt like God "remembered me". I felt like I had a purpose and even at that moment, I asked, "God how could you even use someone like me who has no one and is nobody? Do you ever wonder why it seems as if people know who you are yet you don't even know who you are yet? Sometimes your spirit can make sense of something in the spirit, even when you haven't yet realized it in the natural. This was not by fate or coincidence; this was a divine appointment!

This was a divine appointment set up by God that was ordained before the foundations of the earth. It was a Jeremiah 1:5 moment;

"Before I formed thee in the belly I knew thee; before thou camest forth out of the womb I sanctified thee, and I ordained thee a prophet unto the nations."

There are two important days for a person on earth. The day they are born and the day they find out why! Well, I was already born, but up until now I never knew why! I just took hit after hit. I took whatever life threw at me and tried to adjust and keep a smile on my face. I never once thought, "Is this all for a plan that GOD has for me?" Even though I didn't know, God knew. Jeremiah 29:11 says,

"For I know the plans I have for you, declares the Lord. Plans to prosper you and not to harm you. Plans to give you a hope and a future." (NIV)

I now know that God had a purpose for me and all of my sufferings that I have endured so far are not in vain. I gleaned from this Prophetess for the next couple of years. She saw me through some of the ugliest stages I have ever gone through. We were so close that God would even wake her up in the middle of the night and tell her I was up to no good!

She would always call or text me and say, "Are you behaving?" I would think to myself, "How did she know I was about to do something that I would regret?" I knew what it was though. I tried to run, but the more I did the more she called!
I finally answered my calling and enrolled in the School of the Prophets Training Class, where I learned the basics of who I am to God and the functions of the office I was called to.

Removing the Mask (poem)

Depending on how long you've been masking, it may hurt coming off.

The pain you feel is yourself rejecting the truth.

The truth is, you've been living a lie.

A lie telling yourself;

I'm beautiful. I love me. I love God. I love my family.

I love my boyfriend, girlfriend, husband, or wife.

The truth is, I hate me.

I don't think God can use a person who has no one to depend on, who struggles with low self-esteem, being a role model, lazy, procrastinator.

Pimples. Bad teeth. Fat.

I mask because I don't want people to see me how I see myself, but it has to come off.

While I start to peel away my mask, I see it is taking my skin with it and it's dark.

It smells horrible under there because it hasn't been washed in years.

It's like wearing a cast for twenty years instead of two months.

It smells like rotten flesh.

See, when you wear a masked truth can't enter and where truth can't get in, you die.

Spiritually, once the mask is off you need to be cleansed.

Baptized in truth, mind, body, and soul.

Born again.

Masking makes you reject who God the Father has called you to be.

Allow Jesus Christ to get in and teach you by his Holy Spirit.

Read your Bible.

Find God there and let Him show you His love and His purpose for your life.

Never wear a mask again.

Arise in Your New Beginning

When we went back to the house after church, we talked for hours. I shared with her some of my life struggles and I didn't hold back. For the first time, I felt a connection with a woman that felt like a mom and a friend. I told her the deepest voids in my soul. Growing up, no one ever hugged me or told me they loved me. I started to see tears in her eyes and then she embraced me. For the first time, I felt a release in my heart. She listened to me without judgment. I told her everything I was going through. I felt lonely and afraid. She gave me the best advice. She told me, "God will send people in your life when you need it the most."

I loved my aunt-in-law. She saw deeper than my issues of life. She helped me become a better woman. I remember being sick and God spoke to me and said, "Mind over matter." She was resilient and nothing made her waver. Everywhere she went, from Chick-fil-a to church, she took Jesus and a smile with her. She lovingly took me in as her own. She picked my kids up from school when they were sick, and she would bring me lunch at work; just for us to talk every day. I could be myself. She knew all my secrets and flaws. I felt like the little girl running in a field of grass with her; free. I finally felt I could be free.

God told her to prepare her home for me. I resolved in my heart that there was no way she could do anything to hurt me or betray me. At this point in my life, I didn't have a mother, father, or family. I was scared because it was just my kids and me, along with a few associates. My husband and I were not on good terms, on the verge of a break-up, separation, or even divorce. I started to see a pattern with me. I was okay with letting people go. I just couldn't let everyone go. I always had to have one person with me; for my sanity. Little did I know, God was going to shake my world soon. How many of you know that anything you worship or exalt before God, He will remove? According to Exodus 20: 3-5, God tells us,

"You shall have no other gods before me. You shall not make for yourself an image in the form of anything in heaven above or on the earth beneath or in the waters below. You shall not bow down to them or worship them. For I, the Lord your God, am a jealous God, punishing the children for the sin of the parents to the third and fourth generation."

As I was reflecting on when I didn't have a family, my son's father was there. I worshipped him, but not with my lips; it was my actions. I would allow my son's father to keep me home on Sundays instead of going to church. I stayed home to cook, clean, have sex, or whatever it took to please him. He was content with me doing everything while I laid there at night while I was feeling empty inside. I was always satisfying him, but I was never satisfied.

Five years later, God made me choose my spiritual walk or him. I chose to let my son's father go. Every friendship I spent more time with more than God, ultimately ended with some sort of "misunderstanding". God has a way of getting the attention of the ones He has called and chosen. Over time, my aunt-in-law had become my go-to person and my confidant. I left my husband, eventually, with the help of her counsel, then God removed her too. He allowed me to overhear her saying bad things about me and it hurt me so deeply that I cut her completely off. I was angry and my heart began to harden because the people I loved didn't love me back.

Some people only want God for the issue they are having at that time. Many don't go to the Father for their deeper issues that cause the problems. People only want to treat the symptoms. But God can do both. He wants us to live in total freedom. Knowing this is very important and once you know your purpose and position, you can't let the enemy's tactics and schemes keep you from doing what you are supposed to.

I had to let go of every distraction. Even as I write this book. Many things came to take my focus and I prayed to God to remove the root. The root problem for me was not understanding my level of influence; how important I am to God and the Kingdom. Unfortunately, I entertained the enemy and his distractions which kept me from doing God's will. I truly struggled with my identity, even after removing the mask. I lacked the desire to seek the Father to find out why. After many failed relationships, hurt, self-sabotage, and seeing others close to me reach great success, I finally said, "Enough is enough."

No one will give you everything you need or tell you everything you need to know. Sometimes, you must do your own research and that will require studying, seeking God, fasting, and praying. That's what I did, and you wouldn't believe what happened next; I began thriving. I started obtaining the desires of my heart.

The very thing you struggle with is sometimes the thing God wants to perfect in you! I struggled a lot, even in high school. I failed the writing portion of the ACT, twice. I had to go to a writing class to qualify for graduation. The instructor said to me, "You write how you talk, and it's not good. You're not a good writer." I needed a lot of help just to get the basics. That comment stuck with me for over ten years. It caused me to feed the doubt of becoming an Author. I started having dreams of signing books and I began seeing book titles, but I never thought it was MY book. GOD still used that moment to push me, and it made me want to rely on Holy Spirit more. I trusted Him more. My gift as a writer didn't come from me, but it was placed within me to help those struggling with identifying their self-worth and overcome the tricks of satan. If I had listened to that English professor that day, you wouldn't be reading this book nor would I have ever been able to become successful or a finisher! GOD is strategic. Nothing you face in life is by mistake. It all serves a purpose, and it prepares you for what you will face later down the road.

Take a moment to think of your life path as a long road trip. On this journey, you never know what you will face or who you will meet. Some interactions are divine pit stops, connections to make sure you get what you need, and they also come to validate that you are on the right path. Other interactions may not be so pleasant. Some people are like nails in the road; ready to give you a flat. They want to take the life out of you and slow you down or even cause a wreck. However, you must never let it take you out. You must pull over, call for the right backup, and wait for them to repair your vehicle before continuing your life's journey.

Always remember, every ending is a new beginning. Life is seasonal. When people come into our lives and begin to give us everything we need, we can often pedestalize them instead of giving God the glory. Don't take it personally when a person's season is up. Never forget what they taught you but be willing to let them go. Embrace the goodbye as much as the hello. Just like God brought them, He will bring another. It is all part of God's plan.

Forbidden Yet Addicted

Did you know your spirit can speak to someone before you do? I didn't know until it happened. We locked eyes. There he was. The man I had been dreaming about was standing right in front of me. We locked eyes and we instantly connected. I knew him and he knew me; just not in this dimension. Our connection was orgasmic.

After working together for a little while, he moved onto another job. I thought it would be the end of our connection, until one day I received a phone call that changed my life. "I want you. Now." Now up to this point, we had nothing but an emotional connection. Even though I was married, I still felt so close to this man. When he said that, my heart dropped. We met and talked for about four hours. We laughed, he laid in my lap and told me his secrets, and cried. This is where the vulnerability caused us to collide.

He was my addiction. At the time, I thought this man was heaven on earth. The way he undressed me. We made love for hours every time we met up. His love was electric to my soul. He lit the fire in me. Our chemistry was crazy. When he called, I came. I was willing to leave everything I knew for him. He filled a void in me. How could something that feels so right be so wrong? Letting him go so that my soul could live was the hardest thing had to do.

I didn't want to let him go, but I had to. I had to sober up. I was drunk in my emotions. I was better than a side piece. I was royalty. I was the daughter of a King. How could I let myself fall and become a victim? The love we had was so rare. If I could only get him to say it. He never told me he felt what I felt.

This man was my addiction. Because I refused to deal with my reality of being rejected by the man who was supposed to love me, I fell into the grips of lust, and boy did it have a grip on me. I reached a point in my life where I was done being the good woman. I was the good wife and got cheated on. I was a good person and was constantly being taken advantage of. I was rejected by my adopted family and my real family. I was DONE! I was angry with God. I had taken matters into my own hands. I didn't know the cost. I had dreamed of this man until he became my reality. I heard it in my spirit loud and clear. He was forbidden fruit and I didn't care! He made me feel like a queen while we were intimate. We shared magic. I was his poetry. It was like I was getting high every time I was with him. I only sobered up on my drives home or when I wasn't with him. Yes, I was still legally married, but we were separated, and I was living by myself. I was lonely, scared, hurt, confused, and disappointed. He fixed all of that for me, temporarily anyway.

He needed me to be his nurturer, to care for him. He also needed me to be a friend. I needed a man to love me and give me what I was missing! I loved to self-medicate, but I hated the withdrawal of not being constantly high. Though highly erotic and perfectly passionate, this relationship still didn't give me what I wanted; his heart. I wanted him to say, "I only want you and I'm willing to leave everything for you." One day I had an epiphany that this relationship would always and forever only be sex!

I knew this was not God's will for my life. I lost a part of me that I couldn't ever get back. Not only that, but I also paid a heavy price of falling into a deep depression and gaining over 60lbs. I was tricked out of my position in God all because I was in pain and I refused to deal with it! I learned don't ever fall in love with a distraction. Don't fall in love with someone based on a void or it won't ever work!

As my flesh was being pleased, my spirit was dying because of all the soul ties I was being filled up with. I believed the lies I told myself, "Maybe he was the one, and he had to love me because there was no way this felt like heaven and he didn't." It took me years to be cleansed all because of my moments of pleasure! If things already didn't seem bad enough, he went on to live what seemed to be a happy life and I was left alone to face my truth and be delivered!

When a distraction comes, go back to what you were doing before it came. Right before he came into my life, I was removing the mask and about to deal with all of my truth!
As you heal, I suggest getting counseling, an accountability partner, or talking with a confidant that will lead you back to God's will!

Now that I am healed, I don't take back this learning moment in my life. It taught me never to think that the grass is greener on the other side or try to make your life better by replacing it with someone different. The only way things get better is by facing our reality or truth so we can know what caused the pain and why we are acting the way we do! In this case, I had to forgive myself for falling into temptation because of being vulnerable! I also had to forgive him because he was just as vulnerable as I was. My pain caused me to look at him as the "bad guy". The truth is, he was broken too and he needed deliverance too. I truly hope that wherever he is that he was able to get the healing and deliverance that we both longed for.

It's okay to forgive yourself, I had to. Also, never say what you won't do because if you are not careful you will do it. The flesh is stronger and more powerful than we think. This is why it must be crucified daily.

This was the ultimate betrayal for me. I needed help. I went off the deep end doing things I promised myself I would never do. Everything had finally come crashing down. I couldn't even look in the mirror at one point because I was so depressed and disgusted with myself. I had drifted so far away off the ocean's shore that it took back up from the heavens above to pull me back into safety onto dry ground.

Fruit eaten before it is ripe can be poisonous and ultimately hurt you instead of helping you. Take lychee for example. It's a naturally sweet, floral fruit, but when eaten before it's ripe it can lead to really low blood sugar or even death!

The enemy used my vulnerability to make my desires a reality. If it's not in God's will, it still has the power to manifest and your life can take a turn for the worse. What you ignore now, one day you will have to hear loud and clear. I paid for biting forbidden fruit. I slowly learned that your flesh will always betray you if it's not submitted to Holy Spirit.

When a man and woman lay together a transfer of spirits takes place. By nature, men and women were created to love one another, but within the confines of God's way of doing things. No one really wants to talk about it, but sexual energy is very powerful, and it can bind you to a person's soul. This is why we must be very careful not to allow just anybody to lay with us. That goes for both men and women.

Forbidden Fruit(poem)

I thought I touched the hem of his garment.

I heard his sermons and his gifts.

His wordplay mirrored scriptures like the big book of life called the Bible.

It wasn't long before worship and Lord knows I praised him.

I guess that's how I missed the war ship sailing into my spirit.

Sicknesses from beautiful serpents sucked upon me like leeches.

Soul ties with the soulless.

Feet first and breach position, kicking me out of my father's will.

Who are you?

Because all I know of me is what you left with.

You have me looking for me, in the book of Kings, knowing I was created in Proverbs.

I went from a lady of virtue to Rahab.

Now needing rehab, that I can't afford because I spent myself broke.

Offering you my offerings.

Many times I gave tithes to you, never got my tenfold or 15 minutes of fame.

Do I need to pay for you to see me because you don't?

You never did.

But you did see this body 5'5, thick in the thighs, bedroom eyes, body parts in all the right size.

I made you lose your mind on the inside of me.

I gave you the best of both worlds.

Dropping knowledge on a pillow talk, but you were too busy planning long walks and talking family with all these other chicks.

You know the "better than me chicks".

It doesn't get any better than this chick.

I bet you banked on me losing value in my worth.

Forgetting whose I am, but unlike them did you forget?

I'm plugged into the Creator and while I'm filled back up to virtue I can't get back what you took.

So, love, you can stand for the benediction because you've been evicted.

There won't be another victim that falls victim to your manipulating love.

See me, I'm a daughter of a king, clothed in royalty.

I am divine and baby you can no longer cross this line.

Didn't your mother ever teach you not to play with God!

Bitter and Angry with God!

The day I got upset about it, was the day I changed. I didn't like the way my life was going. The lack of success, repeated failures, being alone, rejection, emptiness, abandonment, and the inability to fit in, was weighing heavily on me. I believed I deserved more.

I was laying in my bed tossing and turning, thinking it was just a night of insomnia. As I laid next to my husband listening to his snoring, I texted my baby sister in Christ and told her to pray for me. I couldn't sleep and it was at that very moment that I heard the spirit of the Lord telling me to pray. Deliverance was coming. I began to weep and weep uncontrollably. I heard the Lord telling me to go into the prayer closet. I laid there and I let out a loud exasperating cry on my back. I heard him talking to me to place my right hand on my belly. I did it and closed my eyes, while tears flowed out. Everything I learned in the prophetic class at church came to my mind. It was about the spirit of bitterness.

I began to see myself in past relationships and I saw how I was always there for people. I would pick up the phone if a friend called and I would give them good advice even if I had just gotten into a fight in my home. I gave them money even if I didn't have money to pay my own bills. Even if they needed food, I fed them.

God began to show me that I became bitter, over time, because I became tired of being used. People would take the good from me and when they were done using me, they would either not call anymore or they would walk away and I would never hear from them again. Something bad would happen, they would say I told a lie on them, or I talked too much, and gossiped. They would also say, I owed them money, which sometimes was true, but I never meant to destroy the relationship.

I didn't ever intend to do anything to end it. God began to show me my marriage. I felt like I should be honored and showed off more in public like the people I see on social media. He showed me when I stepped out on my husband multiple times, I was looking for honor and respect! I wanted to feel worthy! I'm a good woman and there were men out here showing off women who weren't even as classy and respectful as I was.

God showed me that the bitterness spread, and it laid with me at night and it tormented me in my sleep by replaying images of my failed relationships. I saw images of how I gave my all and no one thought I was worthy enough to stay with, not even my husband who laid next to me every day and night. I had to come out of agreement with bitterness. The truth was I felt worthless. Bitterness was spreading like cancer. In every failed relationship the bitterness grew until I felt like there was no cure. This was who I was becoming. Even my physical appearance began to change. My skin complexion changed. I became emotionless and numb. Failure began to set in. My marriage ended. No friends. No family. No church family. Nothing. I began to pray against the root of bitterness. It could not keep me bound any longer. I began to say,

"I speak life to every dead place within me and I command the living water of God to pour into my dead places and cleanse my soul! Every broken promise, word curse, and every form of rejection from anyone that has entered in my life, and crossed my path intending to harm me, I cut ties with it now in Jesus's powerful name; The only name to heal, deliver, and set free. I choose freedom today and it shall be mine!

I urge everyone one hearing or reading this book, to get free now from the spirit of bitterness. It will only hinder the move of God in your life! I pray for freedom, healing, and deliverance to manifest in your life right now. I had so many failed relationships at this point in my life. I tried and tried to put my best foot forward. I seemed to be failing. God was tugging at me, but I was so angry. My health had failed, so my long-term dream of being a nurse was gone! Everywhere I worked after the hospital wasn't good enough. I hated it! I even worked on labor and delivery for a year on the overnight shift. I cried almost every morning getting off. I hated the hours and it wasn't the same. I wasn't happy in my home, I wasn't happy in my heart. I was bitter and I didn't know it then, but I was hitting the rock bottom of life! I learned to smile in public and cry in the bathroom, while being drowned out by running the faucet water! The truth is, I was broken, helpless and I needed Jesus like never before. I contemplated taking pills, but I knew my kids would end up in foster care, so I couldn't just give up like that.

I tried praying, but it seemed as if God had forgotten I exist. God never forgets. He is always there. I needed someone to lay hands on me, therapy, something, anything. I was tired. Well, let me tell you sometimes you don't need any of that. You just need to have a made-up mind that you're tired of letting the enemy control you, your emotions, and your actions. God looks at the heart of a man. Every time He showed up and out in my life, it was because in my heart, deep in my conscious mind, I was ready for him too. There is now a new shift in how God moves. He needs to know you are ready for Him. God won't force the Holy Spirit will upon you. HE IS GOD and GOD alone! He has sent Jesus to conquer everything you are going through, there was nothing too hard for Him. The spirit of the Lord took me into a deep sleep. This is where I saw myself cradled like a baby, crying. The feeling that I had when I was younger came back over me. It was the feeling of needing to be held by my mother. My bitterness came from the womb of not being loved by the woman who birthed me, but in reality, I was angry with God too. I screamed in this vision, "Why God? Why would you let me come to earth and be treated like this! Why couldn't I have a mother or father? Why God? Why did I have to be motherless? I just wanted her to love me." I felt the spirit of God love me in that deep place. Everything changed from that moment.

A sense of peace came over me. I knew I was sent here for a reason. I had a new revelation; you can't break anything you don't face. Many women in my bloodline couldn't win against the enemy because they weren't willing to submit the flesh to God. He knew I could, that's why He sent me here. He knew I was a fighter from birth. I came into this world fighting to survive and I had to fight for anything good. He processed me to overcome the tricks of the enemy. He said, "You are an OVERCOMER!" I woke up, dried my face, and held my head up.

Be the Change (poem)

Be the change you cry about.

Be the change you spend buying a vest.

Invest in yourself.

Before in others.

Be the mirror you check.

Write it before it bounces.

There are so many changes that change you.

You must stay true to you.

Be the change you speak about.

Suffocating the sound you put out.

Don't choke on your words. Spit it out.

Be the change you laugh about knowing it's the same laughter to keep the cries about..face.

You smile about.

Be the fight.

Throw them a left hook. Jabs back at the world trying to take your CHANGE.

Don't let it rob you of your joy, peace, family, finances, or laughter.

Take your change back.

Turn them into dollars.

And dollars into plastic.

And from plastic to diamonds.

Be the change that blossoms from crack pipes

To pipes crack from the pressure.

Be the rose that grew from change lying on the concrete.

Picked up by strangers.

Left and watered by change.

Accept change as it withers the leaves to weather your storms and weather the storms change.

Don't YOU change.

A season may come and go.

A season doesn't last very long.

Once it is done, you taste better.

No one ever liked it bland anyway.

Change taste bitter.

But it spends better once you know what you're selling.

I mean buying.

Change is what you perceive to better not bitter, bigger than you.

Not bitter.

Bitter hardens the change so you cannot exchange love.

God is love and His love is purified by CHANGE in the Holy Spirit.

Pick up this change!

Overcomer

The saying "If I had ten thousand tongues, I still couldn't thank God enough," is very true. So far, you've read about many things that have felt as if it defeated me, but in fact, if it did I wouldn't be writing this book right now. How did I come to this discovery of labeling myself as an overcomer?

Up to this point, I had been through so much, and I still managed to hold my head high, but this was becoming too much. I had become tired and angry. I fled to another city to get a fresh start. While I was running away from them and all the pain I had gone through, I ran right into the person I was most angry with, God. When the Prophet spoke purpose over me, it shifted my whole life. A stripping began.

Though this process was necessary, it was long. God was able to strip away my mask and allowed every hidden seed to come forth. I committed adultery, I churched hopped, I lost jobs, quit jobs, and I quit people! It was time I dealt with my own reality! The spirit of God said to me, "If you don't deal with it at this level when I elevate you it will come out when you least expect it.

I began to see mega Pastors being exposed for molesting children after they have been established in ministry. I knew that God wanted me to see me. I went to sleep one night, and I began to see how people thought about me, I began to see how I really felt about myself. I saw myself being very fearful, anxious, and severely insecure. I also saw myself having low self-esteem, being rejected, angry, lying, lusting, and many other things that weren't of God.

Most people think that when God deals with you, it's always pretty; that's not the case. Just like the woman with the issue of blood, I had to press my way to Jesus. His touch healed me. Healing can be very painful. This was a touch and that caused every UGLY thing inside to surface and I had to deal with each of them, one by one. Over time, God put powerful people in my life to either help uproot things out of me or teach me valuable lessons.

I found a licensed therapist who allowed me to see myself in all of my issues. She also gave me coping methods to deal with the problems, should they arise. She said something so profound that I'll never forget. She said, "I never really met anyone like you. Without a doubt, you are chosen by our Father to be an overcomer. Just remember, we are like pilgrims, we are just passing through. Don't take everything so personally, Diane. You're too close up on your problems. Take a step back and see God in all of the lessons."

I learned the true meaning of being an overcomer. I didn't let it take me out, but instead, it gave an insight into people's hearts, and I've learned to depend on the spirit of God to lead me and direct me. You have to be careful when you're becoming a better person and when you are trying to evolve. Make sure you don't have too many fires burning in your life at one time, because it makes you vulnerable and defenseless to the enemy. The enemy will BECOME whatever your heart desires. I had to learn that the hard way because I was easy access for the enemy. When things aren't good in our personal lives, we tend to look for an outlet that will make us feel better and avoid the pain we are going through.

"Be sober, be vigilant; because the devil walking about like a roaring lion, seeking whom he may devour."
1 Peter 5:8.

Sometimes we drink, smoke, have sex, gamble, binge eat, do drugs, or just simply allow our minds to get caught up with foolish thoughts. As the old folks used to say, "An idle mind is the devil's workshop." Make no doubt about it. The enemy has a kingdom and they are highly ranked in the spirit realm.

I let people and family dictate my place in God for so long that it almost cost me my destiny. I chose to overcome because God had a purpose and a plan for my life also because of the many unmet childhood needs I didn't feel worthy, accepted, supported, or acknowledged. Even though I was young, I could always see through people's masks and fake personalities. Most of the time people didn't know I could see how they really felt about me. I didn't know I was gifted at the time, I just used it as a way to protect myself.

When you have unmet needs as a child, normally you grow up angry or masking your true feelings because it is hard for you to trust anyone with your heart. I had to stop coping and tolerating my pain. I had to be healed. I had to forgive my childhood. I had to say goodbye to the little girl who was dictating my life and controlling my emotions. I had to let her die! But how? First, I had to acknowledge that I was experiencing childhood trauma. It will manifest in many ways. If you're like me, one of the signs was not trusting anyone. I would always find a way to destroy the relationship because I just didn't think someone could love me unconditionally. I found multiple ways to self-sabotage.

As I became an adult, I isolated myself more and more. I was so rejected in my youth, that I went through years of depression. I was always so anxious and fearful. This was another sign that I wasn't in control. I let things that were not God, control my mind, will, and emotions. Once my Father affirmed me and showed me His love, I was able to overcome the spirit of rejection.

I'm grateful that I can go back and speak to young and older women and let them know that even if you didn't get the love or attention you needed in your youth, don't let it keep you from walking and pushing to becoming a better YOU! I always knew I was special. I knew when I walked in any room from the little girl until now that I could light up the room and draw a crowd. I was born to shine God's light and love. I just had to be unwrapped out of my past and processed into my purpose! I am happy to say that I am an OVERCOMER, and you can be too!

Out with the Old, In with the New

Just because you've been knowing somebody a long time doesn't mean they are the right one for you. What do I mean by "for you"? Having your best interest at heart. Some people are close to you, not to get to know you, but to get all the information from you so they can use it against you. There are people in your circle that will never be happy for you no matter how much they've seen you struggle.

There are people that are close to you, who God will reveal, have spirits in them that are like snakes. There are people that will get close to you that will reveal to you that in the beginning, they didn't like you, but now they are getting to know you they love you. No, they don't! That doesn't mean you shouldn't love them or be in a relationship with them. However, the only thing it should do is give you a perspective and insight into how to handle them. It shouldn't make you put them on blast, hate them, or cut them off. Eventually, if they are not really who they are supposed to be, they will fall off.

A few years ago, I was working at a financial services call center. I wasn't in a good place in my life because I had marriage problems. We were on the way to divorce court in my eyes. I was pregnant, and truthfully I didn't want to be pregnant. I met my new manager before coming out of training. Out of thirty people in the training class, I was the only one on her team. I introduced myself and told her a few things about myself including being pregnant. "Wow, well you better take care of yourself." She shared some of her testimony with me with much grief in her tone; she had five miscarriages.

Immediately, there was something that came over me that gave me chills. I didn't know what it was at the time. As time went on, I got really close with her. I had become her assistant. I led her team when she was absent. She often confided in me. She was so confident in me and my abilities to lead that she told me that I was next up to be the manager! She was very supportive and engaging and then something changed.

I noticed her body language changed towards the end of my pregnancy. As I was embracing pregnancy more I became more excited. I had planned a baby shower and invited my closest coworkers, including her. She kept telling me how excited she was for me. The day of the shower came and I looked anxiously for her to come. I got a text from her that she was so sorry but she was extremely exhausted from work that day. She said she would still stop by to give me a card. When she came, I greeted her with a hug and that's when I saw it.

Jealousy overshadowed her smile and took over her body language. She didn't want to be there, she wasn't truly happy for me as she looked at me and my husband celebrate the birth of another child. Sometimes people can't truly be happy for you because of their own disappointments in life. She left that day as quickly as she came and when I returned to work the next day she wanted to know all about it and see pictures. I pondered on what I saw the day before but I second-guessed it and continued showing her everything. Sometimes God will show us who people are and it's up to us to believe it. If you don't, eventually something else will happen to make it more obvious.

A few years went by and I was encouraged by her to stay with her as she was "training me" to be just like her. I had passed up opportunities to transfer out to different departments, just to stay connected to her. I thought because we were close she would look out for me when I had issues come up, so I wouldn't lose my job. That security alone made me miss my opportunity for growth. She knew more about me than most close friends. The more people know about you the more possible bullets it can be to take you out. Above all else, guard your heart, for everything you do flows from it. (Proverbs 4:23)

I'll never forget that morning. I worked from 5 am-1:30 pm. It was around 11 am and my manager had just come back from a meeting. She was handing out papers, and normally she would just take me off the phone to do it, but she didn't. When I received mine it was showing a lot of occurrences that had previously happened on a lot of the days where we had "snow days". I immediately spoke up. I put my customer on hold and I asked, "Why am I getting a point for days I couldn't control? I don't control the weather!" Many of the teammates turned around and started laughing. Some were looking on in complete shock. Their faces said, "I can't believe she just said that." I finished up with my customer and asked to meet with her. With a trembling voice, I said, "Look, I'm on my own at this time. My husband and I are living in two separate homes. You know I can't afford to lose my job. I need to talk to someone."

I was coming from a pure place in my heart. I was truly scared that this was true. She replied with the most evil look on her face. After sitting there pouring my heart out she replied, "If it wasn't for me, you would've been gone because of those sickly kids." I replied, "Do what you have to do then. I'm not going to debate with someone who feels like they are doing me such a favor."

I was extremely pissed. I got up and walked out. While I was packing up my things to leave for the day, she said, "Sit down." I looked at her and said, "I was told if I can't do my job, I have the right to leave (which is a real policy with this company). Today I'm exercising this right." I stormed out the door. Everyone on my team was in shock that I responded this way. She chased me down and pulled me into a room with tears in her eyes. She explained to me how I embarrassed her and how she did so much for me. I explained to her I truly had a concern about my job. I didn't do it to make her look bad. I was upset that she had to give us points for snow days that had nothing to ultimately do with us because we were snowed in. I apologized to her because I hurt her feelings. I offered to go back in there and apologize to the team. I had a bad day and I was dealing with a lot in my personal life. She accepted it, so I thought. I went back to work and sent a group chat apologizing for my behavior, or if I offended anyone. From that day, the relationship between myself, her, and all of my teammates changed. I was off for the next two days. When I came back my desk was moved to the end of the row. This was odd because I had been right next to her for the past few years.

Out of ten of my teammates, I had gotten really close to four of them. I was even able to minister to a few of them. None of them spoke to me that day. The feeling was off, I tried to go on as if it was normal, but the reality is something wasn't right! I spoke to my manager. She smiled and spoke back. We had a meeting that day and I normally assisted with these things. When I got in the meeting, it was about attendance and there was a "new rule"; there will be no more special privileges. Where you are now is where you would stay. Some of my closest friends were cheering her on saying things like, "Yes! No more teacher's pet or excuses about "sickly" kids allowed." "OUCH!" I knew she was talking about me.

It doesn't take a genius to see I was being targeted and she was upset. After a month of no one talking to me and being demoted, unofficially, I wasn't excited about going to work and started to feel bad every time I went in. I went to my doctor and she felt as if I was dealing with depression because of my personal life, work, and church. I wasn't happy in none of those areas. I felt like God was allowing everyone to betray me and I just couldn't figure out why. My Doctor wrote me out of work for a month and told me to start taking meds. I didn't take it, but I did go to see a counselor. She stated I had a lot of jealous and intimidating people in my circle. I also had a lot of fires burning at one time. She told me the only way to get peace is to put out one fire at a time. She told me that I couldn't run from it and that I must deal with it head-on. Lastly, don't compromise. She explained to me that I didn't do anything wrong. I just didn't need to be a pushover. Some people only feel powerful when they have control. I returned to work feeling empowered, refreshed, and unstoppable! However, this time my manager had turned almost everyone on the team against me. Everyone looked at me with disgust. I still smiled and worked super hard. The hate for me pushed me to excel. I was only required to sell five credit cards a month and I did thirty-seven that month!

I was shining and there was nothing she could do. Normally, they will give you recognition, but she didn't. I was being kicked out of the group chat when I logged in. I requested a meeting with HR to switch teams because I knew how I was being treated was against policy. She turned on me and took all of my "supposed friends" with her. I thought taking a month off would help, but it made the hate even worse. Once I returned. She pulled me into the office and said, "While you were gone HR did some kind of odd audit and saw that you missed days from a previous year. I couldn't cover for you and I had to give you points for that." As if I agreed, she continued, "Sign here." I said, "Why are you doing this?" She refused to answer me. I said, "I thought we were better than this?"

It was at this moment that I looked at her and saw the bitter, cold-hearted person that I saw a year ago; I remembered when

I was on the phone and I felt a nudge in my spirit to tell her something. I'll never forget this moment. I whispered over to her and said, "Remind me to tell you something I just heard in my spirit." I was so uneasy that morning. She said, "I can't wait until later. Jump off the phone real quick. She pulled me into a room. I said, "God wanted me to tell you that He wants to heal your heart." God began to minister through me to her about her bitter heart. It was a warning that if she didn't change it may stay that way or end up bad for her. It may push the closest people away. I prophesied things I didn't even know about. I saw tears forming in her eyes. I hugged her and left. I asked if any of it sounded familiar and she said some of it, but my spirit said it was all true she wasn't willing to admit it.

"Pride is the mask of one's own faults." Unknown.

As I signed on that line, I knew my assignment with her was up. I also knew that eventually I would be fired, but it was a part of God's plan. Sometimes God will send people in your life to help you and if you reject the help they will leave. I was sent to help her to see a different perspective on life. She had become bitter over time. She lost both her parents and had multiple miscarriages. She was happily married to her life partner for over fifteen years. Her paychecks were her own personal spending money. She had what seemed to be, the perfect life, the only thing that was missing was her babies. She was angry with God, I had been sent to let her see my life, my past, and my current state. She needed to see how I was able to still love God through it all. We just can't disown the creator because life doesn't go as we planned.

I told her I didn't have a mom, so her giving me so many motherly tips to be successful, could be her calling. She didn't have to work, but she enjoyed it because she was able to help develop so many young adults like me.

Unfortunately, she didn't take heed to the warning. Sometimes who it comes from blinds us to the fact that God could use someone you weren't expecting. I was let go 4 weeks after returning. I was only 3 days away from being promoted to a recruiter. It was a position that I had privately applied for without announcing it to anyone. I didn't leave upset or bitter. I just knew my assignment was done. I messed up by thinking I knew who she really was, when God was showing me the entire time what spirit she operated from.

I am now a small business owner of my own daycare! It set me up for my greater! I would be lying if I said it didn't hurt. It did hurt. That year, God removed all of the relationships I had. By the end of the year, I was completely numb. Even my friend of almost a decade stopped talking to me for a small disagreement. Why am I telling you all of this? There will come a time where you have to go through betrayal, pain, and jealousy! It may hurt, but just know, God has a bigger plan for you. Some of the relationships will never be reconciled and it's okay. You don't have to hate the people involved. Take the lessons with it and grow into a better person.

Relationships should be reciprocated with love, information, secrets, wisdom, and conversations. If someone is just wanting information from you all the time majority of the time, their motives aren't purified and there is an objective behind it, in this case, she didn't want me to see behind her mask. Nevertheless, it worked out for my good and I forgive her!

Black Sheep Walk

If we stay silent about what we go through or what God has brought us out of, we are no better than our enemy and our ancestors. We become very shallow people. I believe in the breath God put in me. I am here to be a truth-teller and to share the goodness of Jesus Christ. I can only do it by being transparent, forgiving those who have belittled me, hurt me, and overlooked me.

My voice and your voice have a sound that is needed at this very time. We are entering into a season where people are not looking for just another Author, Evangelist, Prophet, Minister, spokesperson, or Motivational Speaker. People don't want to just feel good anymore. They are looking for solutions, strategies, blueprints, encouragement, transparency, and truth. People have fallen so far away from God by trying to become their own gods. We put things before Him with idolatry, our time, and wrong motives. I may never understand it, but He has sent me in the earth to go through some things that will forever shape my heart to be like His.

No, I'm not perfect, nor have I ever been, but my heart is pure. I love every person reading this book. I wrote it to let you know that no matter what you have been through be it abuse or being mishandled in families, by friends or lovers, NEVER let it change who God designed you to be. I know that those are some big bold words to say, but I wouldn't say it if it couldn't be done! I have lived through a lot of trauma and tragedy. Some that I haven't even mentioned. I am a living witness, so I can tell you, it can be done!

How? You have to always stay connected to God through a relationship with Him first. He wants your time, He wants your heart, mind, bills, struggles, and pain. Pray every day. Pray when you're hurting. Pray when you're happy. Pray when you're in need. Pray for your enemies. Pray for the homeless. Pray for the oppressed. Pray for the depressed. Most of all, pray for your bloodline to be saved! We are living in a wicked world that won't share with you the keys of freedom, but I am here to tell you that prayer is one of your lifelines to bombard heaven to get everything you need. I didn't get here overnight. Luke 12:48 tells us,

"To whom much is given much is required."

God requires a lot from us sometimes and it's because God chose me before I was placed in my mother's womb. I came into this world fighting for my life and it never stopped! Everything I ever wanted I had to fight for it! I believe in my

155

fight because I believe in you! I could've given up a long time ago, chose to live my life my own way, and stayed in sin. I couldn't because I believed in my fight. All the times that I didn't agree with wrongdoings, mistreatment, abuse, idolatry, lust, and lies was because I was chosen to be set apart to be the leader the people would need! I wrote this book to help pull out the fighter in you! If you're reading this, you've probably fought many battles seen and unseen, just like I have. Why fight and not win? Win in prayer so you can win in life! The enemy doesn't fight anyone that he doesn't deem to be a threat! So again, believe in your fight, believe in a Holy God, believe His plan and purpose for your life. Our life isn't just for us, it is for others. My fight was different than yours and yours may have been different from others, but it doesn't matter. The only thing that holds weight is that you didn't give up. I speak to the fighter in you to never give up.

If you can't find your strength to keep going, look around you, look at the homeless, look at the underprivileged children, look at the widowed, look at the single mother, and lastly look at your own family. They need you to fight! They need you and they need your GOD! He wants to use your story one day to breathe life in others! But first, it must start with you. Oh, Black Sheep, I remove the muzzle from your mouth. You will no longer be ashamed of your fight, your struggle, where you came from, your family, your pain, or your story.

I bind every mind battle, every insecurity, every manner of fear and anxiety, fear of not being successful, fear of dying, low self-esteem, every word curse spoken from anyone in your family or circle that you will never be anything. I loose God's prosperity, you will win. I loose the winds of God from the four corners of the earth. Winds from the north, south, west, and east to blow deliverance on you to heal your deep wounds, your bad memories of the pain, molestation, the physical, mental and emotional abuse! I break the bondage of unforgiveness, lies, untrustworthy people, shame, laziness, procrastination, and the confusion of our identity! You will live on purpose, God's PURPOSE!

Black sheep are usually the ones that are the outcast of the family. Often, they are rejected or perceived as a disgraceful person. These labels can often leave a person isolated and stuck in life. Most die alone and bitter or they live a life that's not pleasing to God because the spirit of rejection makes them feel like they are not worthy to be accepted or loved.

I've always considered myself a people person. You know, easy to get along with, always caring about other people's feelings, and also treating them fairly. As I got older, I realized I was never really accepted by the ones I wanted to be accepted by, nor did I ever fit in. I forced myself to be accepted into other people's circles by being a jokester or by being a "yes" woman.

Ultimately, I was agreeing to what someone says, even if deep down inside I knew I didn't agree. The truth is, all of my life I was rejected. When you deal with this spirit you don't know your worth nor your purpose, so it makes it easy to fall into being someone you're not. This is why it is so easy to wear masks to become someone you were never created to be. I've spent most of my adult years in rebellion against my mother, family, and even friends. I didn't know why at first, but I began to realize there was something deep inside of me growing next to rejection called purpose.

I knew I was valuable even when I couldn't get anyone else to see it. That's why I have partially only been in two relationships. This is why I separated myself from my family because they were always so negative. This is why I separated myself from friends that took my love for granted. I knew that my purpose was to inspire, encourage, and uplift hurting people, especially women. God had planted his love within me at a young age and that seed grew. Even though I had things I inherited from my bloodline, His love overpowered it all.

The seeds parents plant inside of you at a young age most often manifest once you become an adult. Because of the seeds that were planted in me, the journey to self-love and self-care was a difficult one. I didn't realize how much I despised myself. Seeds of low self-esteem and hate were planted in me at a very early age. When I looked at myself in the mirror all I saw was, "You're ugly", "You're not good enough", "You don't have a mother or father," "Nobody really loves you".

I didn't know where to begin, but I knew I had to start somewhere, and writing was my outlet. I let out my pain on my paper. I realized if I didn't submit to God, I was just another disobedient creation and I wanted to be more than that. I knew that I needed healing and deliverance. But first, that meant I needed a deeper relationship with my heavenly Father. I couldn't do what others could do and be totally sold out to God. I would feel so easily convicted or scared, like something bad would happen to me. God's hand was already on my life, I just had to get Him in my heart so that I could be completely sold out. This was my journey to FORGIVE so that I could heal! A lot of times we are like the man in John chapter 9!

As he went along, he saw a man blind from birth. ² His disciples asked him, "Rabbi, who sinned, this man or his parents, that he was born blind? "Neither this man nor his parents sinned," said Jesus, "But this happened so that the works of God might be displayed in him. ⁴ As long as it is day, we must do the works of him who sent me. Night is coming, when no one can work. ⁵ While I am in the world, I am the light of the world." After saying this, he spit on the ground, made some mud with the saliva, and put it on the man's eyes. ⁷ "Go," he told him, "Wash in the Pool of Siloam" (this word means "Sent"). So the man went and washed, and came home seeing. His neighbors and those who had formerly seen him begging asked, "Isn't this the same man who used to sit and beg?" ⁹ Some claimed that he was. Others said, "No, he only looks like him." But he himself insisted, "I am the man." "How then were your eyes opened?" they asked. He replied, "The man they call Jesus made some mud and put it on my eyes. He told me to go to Siloam and wash. So, I went and washed, and then I could see."

We are born blind or born with a fight that is not our own. Just like the boy born blind in this chapter, it wasn't because he was a sinner and he was paying for his parent's sin. No, he was born this way, so that the works of God might be displayed in him! My life is a testament to me being blind and now I'm able to see! I no longer feel sorry for my sufferings. Now I know my sufferings were all for God's hand at work that He may be glorified through my life.

I didn't suffer because of my parents or even anyone in my bloodline. I suffered so God can show you that He is the only one who can heal the brokenhearted, broken in spirit, the spiritually blind, motherless, fatherless, abandoned, rejected, abused, church-hurt, backslider, bitter-hearted, lost, sick, widowed, divorced, and lonely! God doesn't deny that we won't suffer, but He wants us to know the suffering is not being ignored. God's love for us is what we need to go through our sufferings!

"While I am in the world, I am the light of the world." John 9:5

We were sent here to be the light in the darkness. In my sufferings, I found myself being the light to those around me. I even wondered why would I have to always be the strong one, or the one pouring into others and giving to others even if it was my last? Jesus told the man in this book of John 9 to go and wash the mud he put on his eyes at a pool of Siloam(sent) and he did and now can see!

I want every reader to know that there is nothing that happens to you that is not a part of God's plan. I am God's chosen vessel. Every good or bad thing that happened to me may not have made me feel good, but it will all work out FOR my good.

"And we know that all things work together for to them that love God to them who are called according to His purpose." Romans 8:28

It would have been my heart's desire to be one big happy family. I would have liked my children to know their cousins. I would like to have had family gatherings. I would have liked to gather for holidays, birthdays, and graduations. However, that wasn't my portion. However, after having some tough conversations with my sisters we were able to come to some common ground. We're still a work in progress. To date, my conversations with my aunt are kind of brief but I try to pray with her from time to time. I understand this is the best love she can give and I accept it. I have come in contact with my birth aunt and my birth sister and we have weekly check-in calls. I believe I'm complete, I'm loved, and I'm free.

Who would've known this little girl, born to a mother of a crackhead, who had to be detoxed from drugs as a newborn, would inspire many one day? I didn't know my life had a purpose until I had my appointment with destiny. Today is your divine appointment with destiny. You are a trailblazer, you are enough! You are not what happened to you! You are not your bad choices. You are not like your mother, father, or any bad person or thing someone wants to compare you to! You are beautifully and wonderfully made. You have a purpose. I speak to every Black Sheep reading this book, you are not alone and you should never feel that way. God protects and favors you. He will send people along your journey to pour into you and speak life to you.

Although I'm called to the office of a Prophet, you may be a Teacher, Pastor, Evangelist, or even called to the ministry of hair or dance. Whatever God calls you to do, do it well. Do it with the love that God honors. Whatever we do in love and out of a pure place will last the test of time. I wouldn't be where I am if I had bad motives or hated people. I have loved people that hated me, persecuted me, talked behind my back, and treated me poorly. God always came to my rescue. Not because I was always right, but because my motives were pure.

On your journey, you will always have people coming to take your wins or victories your job in life is to continue to fight for it. Don't give up so easily, I started winning when I learned to fight in the spirit and not in the flesh.

"For we don't wrestle against flesh and blood but against principalities, against powers, against the rulers of the darkness of this world. Against spiritual wickedness in high places." Ephesians 6:12

I was never in a battle with people I was in a war with principalities of this world. I was sent to this earth to break the generational cycle that occurred in my bloodline. You can't break anything if you don't face it. I had to face the demon of abandonment, orphan, rejection, fear, lust, and perversion, anger, bitterness, lies, brokenness, rebellion, and poverty. I had to fight them all with the power of God. He knew I would need help fighting. At the tender age of 14 when I moved to SC on a Wednesday night, I walked into my church a rebellious teenager simply following my friends to the altar, never knowing when I arose that I would arise with the power to help break the generational cycles that were operating in my families lives.

Now I know I'm in his will and He has always had a bigger plan to allow me to see Him in every aspect of my life. I want to encourage you today. You will WIN in life! I prophesy that everything that held you back in the past won't hold you back any longer! I decree and declare to every black sheep; come out of hiding and tell your truth! Even if it's ugly. Even it was painful. Even if you are ashamed of it! I loose the chains of bondage over your mind. You are free because Jesus sent His son to make us free. I am unapologetic about what I went through. Because of it, I am resilient. I am strong. I am an overcomer. I am a finisher. I am whole in Jesus. I am more than enough. I am beautiful. I am loved and so are you!

I am now divorced. I am an amazing mother to 3 wonderful children. I can now call and communicate with all my living family members and I don't have any more bitterness towards them because of the way I was treated. I am not perfect, but I do my very best at making sure that God is glorified with my lifestyle. It took me a very long time to believe that God wanted to use me. With the long battle of knowing my worth, I am now very honored that God has chosen and called me. When He called me He also qualified me. I've been processed for such a time as this. I will share my pain, joy, wins, and losses with the masses. I will help break generational curses off of you with the power invested in me! I have words to heal, words to deliver one wound at a time through my storyline!

If we do what we are commissioned to do in this world, Jesus will restore our sight and we will become unrecognizable! This is what happened to me, I went from being the victim, the lost little girl, the orphan, the abused, the motherless, and now I am God's Prophet, Pastor, and Evangelist. I was sent here to be the light to a dying world and through me, the Holy Spirit lives, granting me the authority to open the blinded eyes! I pray this book blesses your life. Jesus is real and God's hand has been on my life since I came into this world. I am a living testimony of what God has and can do if you let Him!

Black Sheep, walk into your DESTINY, unapologetic of what has happened to you because you were sent here on assignment to love others as your Father in heaven loves you! Jesus came so that we can have life and have it more abundantly. Don't you dare give up on your process. Let God fully process you so that you can be ready for the people you are assigned to. I didn't get here overnight. I've always had a purpose before meeting anyone that caused my pain, and so do you! May you be restored, redeemed, and given back double for all of your troubles. Remember the shepherd, Jesus leaves the 99 for the one which is lost. Black sheep, you are not alone. Jesus has found you!

Black Sheep,

You are a living testimony! Thank you for taking
the time to read and relate to my journey. On
the following pages, you will find a few
questions to help you reflect on your journey,
along with some prayers that will help you
connect with God and take authority over your
bloodline so that you can be truly healed and
walk in your divine authority. Take your time to
reflect on each question. Take your time to pray
each prayer. Remember, it's not just about the
destination. It's about the journey. Allow the
Holy Spirit to guide your pen to answer the
questions so you can have true divine revelation.

Diane M. Mahone

<u>Reflection</u>

1. How would you define your relationship with your mother? In what ways, if any, could it be better?

_____

_____

_____

_____

_____

_____

_____

_____

_____

2. How would you define your relationship with your father? In what ways, if any, could it be better?

_____

_____

_____

_____

_____

_____

_____

_____

_____

<u>Prayer</u>

Father,

I want to be loved by you and I want your spirit to flow in me, Lord. I want to be used by you. I'm tired of fighting against your will for my life. I accept your will and way for my life. I pray that if I am fighting generational curses, I ask that you equip me with your power to resist the enemy so he can flee from me. Open my eyes to the deceptive practices of the evil one. Give me the boldness to speak against lifestyles that directly impact my bloodline. I ask that you will bless everyone connected to me with a 100 fold return. Thank you for healing me from the top of my head to the sole of my feet. From this day forward I walk in your divine healing.

In Jesus name,

Amen

<u>Reflection</u>

1. Define generational curse breaker.

   _____

   _____

   _____

   _____

   _____

   _____

   _____

   _____

   _____

   _____

2. Where can you identify generational curses in
   your bloodline?

   _____

   _____

   _____

   _____

   _____

   _____

   _____

   _____

   _____

__Prayer__

Father,

We thank you for what you have done. We release forgiveness to every parent, parental figure, or guardian that has not given us what we needed growing up. We forgive those who took advantage of us sexually when they were supposed to cover and protect us. Fill any voids that were not filled. We will not charge you, God, for what we did not receive. We ask that you fill us today with your spirit and remove anything that is not of your will. Remove anger, low self-esteem, lust, perversion, rejection, pride, and abandonment. Remove any arrested development or anything that is hindering us from maturing and growing in you. Cover our children as we raise them in your word. Help us to be great examples of parents in the kingdom. Help us to love our children the way you have loved us with grace, mercy, and much patience.

In Jesus name,

Amen

Reflection

1. How do you own your story?

_____

_____

_____

_____

_____

_____

_____

_____

_____

_____

2. How do you address your abandonment issues?

_____

_____

_____

_____

_____

_____

_____

_____

_____

_____

Prayer

Father,

We ask you to cleanse us from any plagues from our forefathers, all the way back to Adam and Eve. I ask that you bind and break every spirit of addiction, perversion, rebelliousness, bitterness, anger, lack, poverty, maliciousness, lust, perversion, diabetes, high blood pressure, rejection, gout, cancer, bipolar, schizophrenia, ADD, ADHD, deafness, anxiety, depression, oppression, fear, doubt, spiritual barrenness, the spirit of the orphan, rejection, confusion and any afflictions in our body because of what was passed down through the bloodline. Wash the bloodline now in Jesus's name. God, I ask that you cleanse us in our mind. Go in our subconscious and heal our memory so that we won't harbor unforgiveness. Thank you for removing the shackles off of our feet and allowing us to be free to be who you have called us to be.

In Jesus name,

Amen

Reflection

1. How do you manage stress?

   _____

   _____

   _____

   _____

   _____

   _____

   _____

   _____

   _____

2. Who do you need to forgive? Write down their names and forgive them one by one.

   _____

   _____

   _____

   _____

   _____

   _____

   _____

   _____

   _____

<u>Prayer</u>

Father,

In the name of Jesus, I ask that you come into my heart right now. Remove every stone blocking my heart to forgive now. Father, I forgive my mother for not loving me the way I needed to be loved. I forgive my father for not being there to love me unconditionally. Father, I ask that you make my heart a heart of flesh to open up to love you more and to love those around me. I ask that you remove the novocaine that makes me numb. I come out of agreement with the child in me that wants to control my emotions. I am no longer an orphan. I am adopted as a child of God in sonship. Ephesians 1:5 reads, "He predestined us to adoption as sons through Jesus Christ to Himself, according to the kind intention of His will." Help me to know every day, regardless of the acceptance of this world, that I am accepted in your kingdom.

In Jesus name,

Amen

<u>Reflection</u>

1. What are some red flags you have learned about relationships that can help you in the future?

_____

_____

_____

_____

_____

_____

_____

_____

_____

2. What are some signs of a healthy relationship?

_____

_____

_____

_____

_____

_____

_____

_____

_____

_____

<u>Prayer</u>

Father,

Thank you for the freedom to reach our destiny. Thank you that we are washed in your blood. Thank you for breaking cycles of going in circles and cycles of not becoming who you predestined us to become, before the foundations of this world. Thank you for our God-given authority. Thank you for giving us boldness to be the light as we walk through the valley of the shadow of death. Thank you for the boldness to stand and speak your word. Thank you for the increase, favor, and abundance. Thank you for the wealth that is laid up for the just. We thank you that we are full of life and love. Our hands are blessed, our children are blessed, and our children's, children are blessed.

In Jesus name,

Amen

Reflection

1. In what ways do you notice "The Black Sheep" arising in you?

_____

_____

_____

_____

_____

_____

_____

_____

_____

_____

2. How can you encourage others to embrace their identity as "The Black Sheep"?

_____

_____

_____

_____

_____

_____

_____

_____

Prayer

Father,

I pray that every generational curse-breaker reading this book breaks every curse and cycle that is holding them captive right now in Jesus's mighty name! I bind the spirit of abandonment, orphan, and rejection. I loose the fire of God to burn away any desires that are not the desires of our Father in heaven. I pray every tormenting demon from your past is cast out now in Jesus's name. You will have peaceful sleep and a successful life. Everything you touch turns to gold. Whatever you put your hands to in this season, shall prosper. Any spirits of lack that may have attached themselves to your bloodline must be cast into the sea, right now. We break every spirit of poverty off of our families. We walk in abundance and prosperity from this day forward.

In Jesus name,

Amen

About the Author
Diane M. Mahone

Diane M. Mahone, a native of Queens NY, now resides in Greenville, SC. She is a mother of 3, author, certified life coach, daycare owner, and minister of the gospel. Diane is passionate about helping women discover their power and strength through God's love. Her hobbies include writing, volunteering, and helping the less fortunate. Diane is anointed to break generational cycles, break strongholds, and administer healing and restoration.

Follow Diane M. Mahone on social media!

FB @ diane.m.gayle

IG @ blacksheepwalk

Book cover design by Alexis Rolley

FB@ THECRE8VEBOSSBRAND

IG @THECRE8VEBOSS

Scripture references KJV unless otherwise indicated

Made in the USA
Columbia, SC
25 June 2021